HAPPINESS 3.0

WHEN ARTIFICIAL INTELLIGENCE MERGES WITH HUMAN HAPPINESS

SID CHATTOPADHYAY

Book title: Happiness 3.0: When Artificial Intelligence merges with Human Happiness

Author: Sid Chattopadhyay

TABLE OF CONTENTS

CHAPTER 1

The Evolution of Happiness

The CEO and the Gardener

When I was a child in the late 1980s, I once heard an interesting story. There is this CEO of a company who sits on the top floor of a multistoried building. He is busy all day, works hard to succeed in his career, and leads a purposeful, active, and stressful life. Every morning, he would observe the gardener come by to tend to the landscaping in the front yard. The gardener would mow the lawn for half an hour. Then, he would unroll a mat he carried with him, spread it, and sleep till noon. After that, he would bring out his lunch box, eat his lunch, trim a few hedges for another half an hour, and then lie down on his mat and sleep again. After a few hours of sound sleep, he would get up, stretch, roll up his mat and go home. He would repeat this every day. After observing this routine for several weeks, one day, the CEO summons the gardener and asks him, "Why do you work so little and just sit around and waste your time all day?"

"Then what?" asks the gardener politely.

"What do you mean, then what!" exclaims the CEO, "You could finish your work in the morning and then work at some other place in the afternoon and evening instead of lying around all day wasting your time."

"Then what?" asks the gardener again.

"Well, if you work at multiple places, you can earn more money and maybe even start your own business."

"Then what?"

"After you have your own business, you can hire other people to work for you and grow your business further."

"Then what?" continues the gardener.

"Well, once you have earned enough money by growing your business, you can relax and just be a happy man!" exclaims the CEO.

The gardener gives him a long look and says, "So, what do you think I am doing now?"

This story amused me at that time. The full circle of a journey to obtain Happiness as a destination, instead of being happy at the current moment and not taking the arduous journey to reach the same destination eventually, was carefully hidden in the innocuous little story.

This story made me wistful too. The gardener's life seemed ideal for a little boy hoping for the rains to come so that school could be off that day and he could play around and do nothing. How lovely not to have school and play around all day in the rain and the mud! That would be such a happy occasion!

I could not help but wish that my life was like that of the gardener: laze around all day, be relaxed, and not be stressed. No homework. No tests. No fear of failure. No judgment on acumen. No expectations. No peer pressure. No competition. Just have ample time to do exactly what I wanted to do all day. Like an endless summer vacation forever. Won't that be simply marvelous? Wouldn't I be the happiest little boy in the World?

Over the last three decades, as I gradually let go of my carefree childhood and embarked on a journey to adulthood, I have realized the complexity of pursuing Happiness. Should one embark on a journey to pursue Happiness, whatever it may be, like the gardener, in some sense, is trying to do? Or should they embark on a journey of pursuing success, combined with all their duties as an individual in this World, with a strong purpose and direction, and hope that Happiness will follow suit, somewhat similar to what the CEO is trying to do?

From wisdom passed on to us through generations, a reasonable path to Happiness is to pursue a set of activities that not only sustain us to navigate life, but make us happy too. Society has evolved that way. There are established frameworks to have a reasonably happy life; as a child, pursue education; as an adult, settle into a system of work, community, family, and friends to somehow float along the river of life and mostly try to be happy. This framework is broad enough to fit most humans. The gardener fits into this framework, and so does the CEO.

Although such a framework is apparent and deeply rooted in how humans have evolved into social beings, the critical metric that created this framework is possibly not to optimize Happiness. Instead, it is to increase the chances of survival on our planet, survival as individuals, and survival as social beings. Let's look at this aspect in some more detail.

Evolution did not favor Happiness

Our planet seems to have evolved with a limited supply of Happiness. The chances of everybody being happy for the same set of events and circumstances seem low. There appears to be a competition to achieve Happiness and, at times, a struggle to hold on to it and not let it get stolen. Competition happens primarily due to the inherently competitive nature of humans. Competition is the key to sports, career, education, social position, or any other facet of a human's life. Competition has permeated into every aspect of life. Resources are so limited that competition seeps into almost every part of life.

If you are a student, you are always competitive; there are limited seats in top Universities; you have to be very competitive and do the right things at the right time to get admitted to the University of your choice with the discipline you want to study. In your career, if you are unaware of what others are doing, others will push you out and get promoted. You will likely be alienated and become an outcast if you don't compete for the correct social circle. Competition extends further to even trivial aspects of life; if you don't book your vacation at the right time, chances are you will have difficulty finding the flights, hotels, and all that goes into the vacation.

Competition for survival is not just a social construct; humans seem competitive biologically. It starts at the very birth; the most agile and the most able, fit, and fastest male sperm gets to go and fertilize the female egg to create the zygote and the new life form. Competition to get ahead is hardwired in our DNA. The structure of society subtly encourages competition, be it materialistic or some abstract idealism.

Sometimes, competition becomes the key even when it is not required. Materialistically, the effects are subtle yet tangible: a small or modest house may not suffice if others have a larger home; a simple car may not suffice if others have better cars; a simple vacation may not suffice if others have more fun vacations, a simple wedding ceremony may not suffice if others had a more lavish wedding.

Competition, however, does not stop at materialistic manifestations. Even the most minor interactions can get competitive. A desire to get attention in a social gathering can be competitive. At work, in society, or any such human constructs, subtle power play continues to be a motif in people asserting dominance or superiority over each other. Even with family, sibling rivalry happens, essentially driven by humans' hardwired tendency to compete and dominate.

These competitions need not always be required for survival. Yet they occur because it seems humans are hardwired to be competitive.

The effect of competition on Happiness is somewhat discernable. The one behind in the competition is unhappy. The one ahead in the competition is relatively happier. That's how we are hardwired.

From all this, and given the biological nature of humans to compete for superiority, we can conclude that humans are **not** designed to be happy naturally! We have to work for our Happiness. It does not come organically or automatically. From prehistoric human forms to modern humans, our evolution was not characterized by increasing Happiness.

What drove evolution?

The evolution of humans over millions of years has been marked by growing skills to fight against hostility across various forms; hostility from predators, from natural forces, and amongst each other.

As humans evolved, some periods were marked with dramatic inventions. Humans' controlled use of fire is believed to have begun around 2 million years ago. The agricultural revolution happened approximately 10,000 years ago when humans transitioned from a hunter-gatherer lifestyle to settled agriculture. The domestication of plants and animals allowed humans to establish permanent settlements, develop complex societies, and create surplus food, leading to population growth and specialization of labor.

The invention of writing systems was a crucial development in human history. Writing enabled the recording and preservation of knowledge, facilitating the accumulation and transmission of information across generations. The Industrial Revolution, which began in the 18th century in Great Britain and later spread worldwide, marked a significant turning point in human history. It brought about a shift from an agrarian society to an industrialized one, with advancements in manufacturing, transportation, and technology. The Industrial Revolution fueled urbanization, increased productivity, and led to dramatic social and economic changes.

In the last few centuries, numerous technological advancements, such as the invention of the steam engine, electricity, automobiles, airplanes, computers, and the Internet, have revolutionized human life. These developments have improved communication, transportation, healthcare, and overall quality of life. They have also led to increased globalization and interconnectedness among people worldwide.

Every dramatic change in how humans developed marked a period of human evolution. What was the key driving force which made humans keep improving and evolving? Happiness? Probably not.

Optimizing Happiness was not the key factor that led to humans' remarkable evolution and development. Instead, the key metric force that drove all this was the instinct of humans to conquer the planet, and make the most out of it, to advance further and further away from other life forms on this planet.

An abundance of Happiness

From the arguments above, increasing Happiness was perhaps a byproduct, but not the essential goal of evolution. Yet, even if evolution possibly did not optimize for Happiness, Happiness, paradoxically, is omnipresent and abundant. The smallest interactions, the smallest hopes, make us happy.

As a child, small things and interactions gave me abundant joy; be it interacting with my friends at school or playing cricket in the evening with local boys, or taking the two-day-long train journey from the West coast of India to the East coast of India to stay with my cousins and extended family for a couple of months during the summer vacations. Happiness was laden in each new cassette of my favorite musical artists, which I bought out of pocket money. Happiness was loaded in the delicious food I had, in the birthday parties on the terrace with friends, in the evening strolls, in pretty much everything. Growing up, like most of us, I get joy from my family, work, hobbies, friends, and perusal of arts, music, and literature. I am sure this was like this, and still is, for most of us.

Happiness also seems to be somewhat arbitrarily distributed. It scales from individuals to entire nations. It pans across genders, races, age, and nationalities. One would expect Happiness, like natural resources on this planet, to be logically distributed and predictable as expected: hot weather around the equator, sand and cacti in deserts, rain in rainforests, cold during winter, hot during summer, coconut trees in tropical places, sweet mangos, tigers having stripes, fish living in the water. Yet, the planets' explainable laws and traits become difficult to extend when it comes to human Happiness. A seemingly happy person who seems to have everything may be bitterly unhappy. And vice versa. An unhappy wealthy person vs. a happy, not rich person. The variations and unpredictability of who should be happy and who not seem to defy a common framework of Happiness.

It looks like even nature is more predictable than human nature and their Happiness.

Evolution of Happiness

Along with human evolution, Happiness has evolved too. What it meant to be happy for a previous generation may not suffice for the next generation. Also, the modes of obtaining Happiness vary across time. One can draw some parallel between the evolution of Happiness and the evolution of humans, especially regarding the technology they use. With every new era of technological advance, shifts of Happiness happen. We do not have anecdotal evidence, but we can theorize.

The invention of (or the discovery of the use of) fire made humans feel much safer against predators and gave them a much broader food choice. The invention of the wheel must have made life much easier than before in terms of transportation and everything associated with it. Each era, be it agriculture and domestication of wild animals or industrialization, brought around a shift in modes of obtaining Happiness or, perhaps, the perception of it.

In recent years, the key technological advancement that changed over successive generations, at least in the last few decades, is the advent of digital technologies. The sudden advent of digital technologies such as smartphones, the Internet, and the Information that comes with it, has radically changed human consciousness and awareness of what is possible. With these technologies, implementing the traditional Happiness framework has become complex. Digital technologies are not just tools anymore, as they were some decades ago. They are an essential part of our lives.

With the advent of digital technologies, the pursuit of Happiness has become much more complex. It has, for me, and possibly for most of us. What digital technologies have provided is a significant shift in Information and awareness. Awareness, obtained through Information, plays a vital role in affecting Happiness. There is dramatically more Information about anything and everything, whether you need to know it or not. Information creates sudden awareness about things you would have never looked up organically.

The relationship between information and Happiness can be complex and context-dependent. Let's look at this aspect in some detail.

Information, awareness, and Happiness

Acquiring information and knowledge about oneself, the World, and various topics can empower individuals to make informed decisions, pursue meaningful goals, and take actions that align with their values. This sense of empowerment and autonomy can contribute to greater Happiness and fulfillment. Being informed about social issues, current events, and the experiences of others can foster empathy, compassion, and a sense of social connectedness.

When individuals are aware of the challenges faced by others, they may be more motivated to contribute to positive change, engage in acts of kindness, or support causes they care about. These actions can enhance Happiness by promoting a sense of purpose, altruism, and social well-being.

Information can give individuals a broader understanding of available opportunities, career paths, lifestyles, and options. This awareness can enable people to make choices that align with their interests, values, and aspirations, leading to a greater sense of Happiness and fulfillment in their chosen pursuits.

At the same time, awareness about some issues can cause distress. As they say, "Ignorance is bliss." Let's look at a simple example to demonstrate this. Jane goes on a vacation to Cancun in Mexico with her family. A few decades back, when smartphones and social media were not around, awareness about her vacation would have been limited to probably the few people she told it to. But now, in this age of smartphones and social media, Jane posts her vacation pictures on a social media platform. Many of her friends, acquaintances, friends of friends, and friends of acquaintances from all over the World, get to know about her vacation through social media and see the pictures of how happy she is on her vacation.

Now, one of Jane's friend's friends, say Mary, sees the pictures, and it affects her largely; because maybe she was planning to go to Cancun but can't, for whatever reasons; be it may be because she cannot afford it, or she doesn't have time or any such things. Mary gets unhappy just because she saw Jane and her family flaunt their wonderful Cancun vacations on social media.

Unwanted Information pushed to us

The serendipity of Information, pushed to our faces even when we did not actively seek it, is the hallmark of the effect of digital technology; with it comes passive awareness about events, things, and other aspects that directly affect our Happiness. In our example, Mary did not have to see or hear about Jane's vacation. But most internet content these days is personalized and meant to optimize engagement; as a result, she ended up seeing it.

There could be an alternate outcome too. Perhaps Jane's vacation at Cancun gave Mary new ideas and awareness about beautiful resorts and beaches that she was unaware of. Perhaps Jane's vacation pictures gave Mary a new impetus to make that vacation happen. The serendipitously lean-back awareness created new dimensions of Happiness for Mary, despite her not seeking it or being close to Jane.

Whatever the outcome is, with the advent of omnipresent digital technology, the pursuit of Happiness has become complex compared to times before the millennium, when digital technologies were in their infancy or even non-existent.

During my student years till high school in the mid and late 1990s, there was hardly any influence of digital technology; neither for me, nor for any of us who were present in that era. During those times, there was very little chance of Mary knowing about Jane's vacations unless she heard it from her directly, somebody in common, or heard serendipitously from some source directly by word of mouth.

It was very different and far simpler back then. It was an era when awareness about anything and everything that could affect Happiness was boxed in books, T.V. channels, radio channels, newspapers, magazines, and occasional anecdotal word-of-mouth knowledge sharing from friends and relatives, and parents.

It was the era of classic Happiness 1.0.

Happiness 1.0

Happiness 1.0 was the sole version of Happiness till the mid-1990s before computers and the Internet became mass available. Happiness 1.0 was directly affected by the boxed source of awareness and stimulation. When Happiness 1.0 thrived, there was no YouTube, WhatsApp, Facebook, Instagram, Google, Pinterest, LinkedIn, Minecraft, online news portals, ChatGPT, Bard, or anything remotely related to the Internet, smartphone, or computer technology. Happiness was not affected by serendipitously obtained stimulants or Information from digital sources.

Until the mid-1990s, when I was in high school, there were inland letters my grandfather used to write long letters to me in his sprawling handwriting instead of emails.

Instead of WhatsApp, my friends got together in person every evening to frolic around, and decided on the time and place where we would meet next.

Instead of YouTube, we used to wait the entire week for the weekend to watch our favorite television cartoons and series.

Instead of Netflix, we could hire VCRs from the local VCR shop to watch our favorite movies repeatedly.

Instead of Google Bard or ChatGPT, we had the school and local libraries where we could dig up Information on topics if we wanted to.

Instead of Google Maps, we had printed Maps we took while traveling.

Instead of Facebook and Instagram, some aunties had daily Kitty parties where they gossiped about everybody and anybody, showed each other pictures of their vacations and kids, and compared their dresses which they bought at a discount.

Unspoken formula

There was an unspoken formula for Happiness 1.0. At that time, it seemed that Happiness 1.0 was prescribed and solved; society laid out plans for how to be happy, with the key source of Information shared by direct actions, direct words, and person-to-person interactions.

The momentum for the methods to be happy was passed on from parents, relatives, friends, teachers, social circle, and occasionally, books, radio, and television. The Information required was obtained from combined wisdom from thousands of years of evolution.

We did not question this wisdom and 'norms' because these recipes for Happiness and well-being were passed on to us through our social and family circles from one generation to the other. The recipe for Happiness 1.0 looked optimal, perfected over generations, with ample evidence that people who followed this recipe were generally happy.

Happiness 1.0 was not personalized. It was a social construct, with norms set by society. There were norms about expectations, career choices, and grownup duties; social hierarchies and patriarchies were set in stone, with gender-based norms and expectations set in quasi-rules. Deviations from the normal were frowned upon.

Happiness 1.0 persisted for thousands of years, weaving its way delicately through the history of humanity; from the first prehistoric baby steps to the iron age to the industrial revolution till the end of the twentieth century; a steady, linear trajectory, piercing through cultures and times, solidly supported by common wisdom and combined human intelligence accumulated over centuries of throttled Information passed on from generations.

A broken line

The linear line of Happiness 1.0, drawn over centuries, had a fundamental problem. Happiness 1.0 was so sandboxed out of information channels that the larger World and the somber buzz of humanity around the World went unheard.

I, for example, did not get to see or hear first-hand Information about the darker aspects of oppression, the real stench of poverty, the pain of broken hopes, atrocities and destruction from wars, and the continuous domination of one group of people over the other—the first-hand Information needed to be included.

What did reach me, and possibly to most of us, was a vague notion of these aspects of humanity, filtered through opaque information methods that came with Happiness 1.0. Information to create awareness about all this was boxed in a few T.V. and radio channels, some textbooks, newspapers, and magazines (for those who cared to read), and colored third-hand Information from very few human connections who were more immersed in the World than we were.

Happiness 1.0 resided in this little sandbox, which was disconnected and isolated. This sandbox, influenced by a narrow set of information-providing entities, was characterized by limited awareness. These information channels were contained, controlled, and one-way. Ordinary people had no say or opinion unless they went extreme to demonstrate physically, resorted to anti-social activities to get noticed, or spoke through their pen at max.

The view of the World in this little box was set by political powers, book authors, ancestors who had a fixed idea of what the next generation should do, friends who were equally starved for quality knowledge and awareness, and a society that had a preset view of what each human was supposed to do.

The broken line of Happiness 1.0 carried forward in the semi-darkness of the confining, at times stifling, box for centuries. The oppressive and dark box of Happiness 1.0, though, did not remain closed forever; it was broken open dramatically over just a few years when human beings, at large, started getting access to the computer and the Internet and everything magical that came with it.

Birth of the Computer and the Internet

As humankind remained confined within the sandboxed Happiness 1.0 till almost the end of the twentieth century, somewhere on this planet, in small labs, institutions, and in the minds of some brilliant people, two radical forces created by humans were being developed in parallel starting around mid-twentieth century; one, the computer, and the other, the Internet. These two technologies rapidly advanced to a stage in the 1990s when they would join hands to change the landscape of awareness completely.

As a borderline millennial child, my journey to adulthood coincided with dramatic strides in advancing these two core technologies. When I was in elementary school in the mid-1980s, several important digital technological events were happening around the World. In 1981, IBM introduced its first personal computer, the IBM P.C., which quickly became the industry standard and helped to establish the personal computer as a mainstream technology. A few years later, in 1984, Apple introduced the Macintosh computer, the first commercially successful computer to use a graphical user interface (G.U.I.) and a mouse. Just a year later, in 1985, Microsoft released the first version of Windows. This graphical operating system would eventually become the dominant operating system for personal computers. In that same year, the first CD-ROM drives were introduced, which enabled storing large amounts of data and multimedia content on a single disc, allowing an era beyond cassettes.

A few years later, in 1989, British computer scientist Sir Tim Berners-Lee created the World Wide Web (W.W.W.). Berners-Lee envisioned a system that would allow scientists around the World to share Information and collaborate on research projects easily. The first web browser, called

WorldWideWeb, was developed by Berners-Lee in 1990. That paved the way for the modern Internet.

After completing high school, when I went to the Indian Institute of Technology (I.I.T.) in 1997 for undergraduate studies in Mathematics and Computing, the Internet, popularized by Tim Berners-Lee in 1990, had already entered the mainstream. I realized that the Internet had the potential to completely change my life when I saw the Internet for the first time at I.I.T. in 1997 when I visited www.yahoo.com using a web browser. Yahoo gave me blue website links to find what I was looking for. I was awestruck at the tremendous power of search engines to create awareness on the Internet.

My discovery of the Internet in 1997 completely and radically changed my life forever. The blue lines from Yahoo's search engine took me to a whole new world of Information and awareness. The websites that Yahoo (and very shortly later, Google) took me dazzled me, as did the entire concept of the Internet. Each query led to a torrent of web surfing, navigating recursively to other websites, making it a delightful experience, almost like an addiction.

I had officially delved into the ocean of awareness created by the Internet, entangled with it to the point of no return. It changed my perception of the World we lived in completely. And with this new tool in hand in the late 1990s, I, and millions like me all over the World, stepped into Happiness 2.0.

Happiness 2.0

The dazzling aspect of discovering an entirely new world through the Internet was powerful to me when I first saw it in 1997 and perhaps to all of us who started realizing the tremendous potential of the Internet. These websites opened a Pandora's box of Information, views, opinions, and life directions. Most importantly, the Internet increased my awareness manifold. There were insights into how the World, society, and humanity worked, insights that were not passed on or discussed by my friends, family, ancestors, or other forms of human knowledge and intelligence.

For the first time in my life, through the Internet, I was in control of what I wanted to know, not what others told me. Suddenly, organic Information became a thing of the past; Information was not to be found from narrow sources; instead, it could be sought out, seen, heard, and felt like never before.

With the Internet, I could escape from the reality of my immediate connection with friends and peers at college and the combined wisdom I acquired from them. My Happiness was not always entangled with other humans or tasks for the first time. This magic new thing, the Internet, took me to far-off places and realms of Information Horizon that I could not even imagine existed.

For all of us who discovered the Internet in the mid and late 1990s, we could detach from real life and plunge ourselves into the sparkling World of the World Wide Web. The World Wide Web presented to us insights that we never thought existed. All these insights were carefully laid out before us, like alternatives to the source of truth we had hitherto known, and gave new ideas to question and challenge them.

For the first time, I could step out of the sandbox where I had spent my entire youth before college. The closed, semi-dark, and stifling little box which contained Happiness 1.0 broke into pieces the moment I could access the vast World and its ways through the Internet. With the advent of this new friend of humanity, I—or all of us who started using the Internet—could step out of the stifling and semi-dark box containing Happiness 1.0 and discover a new form of Happiness: **Happiness 2.0.**

There was a reason young people like me developed a keen passion for web surfing in the late 1990s when we discovered the Internet.

We were inherently discovering Happiness 2.0 and living in it.

We read articles online, played online games, made friends all over the World, sent emails, chatted, and discovered new hobbies. We also became much more aware of International issues, read internet articles by free-minded people, searched for academic content to aid in our college academia, found new places to visit, new languages to learn, new music to listen to, new ideas to think about, and all sorts of things which would have been impossible without the Internet. Every one of these interactions through the Internet increased our awareness of the world manifold.

With it, we discovered new ways and content to make us happy.

This new form of Happiness started getting introduced into the mainstream over the millennium as a fundamental form of Happiness and a mutated and latest version of its original, Happiness 1.0. Happiness 2.0, wrapped around a serene core of global knowledge neatly structured and presented by the Internet through search engines, was an advanced version of Happiness 1.0, a new-millennium mutation of its predecessor.

Happiness 2.0 did not automatically take narrow dictations from just the surrounding humans or narrow and limited "wisdom" and directions set from generations of practices to be happy. The syllabus to stay happy passed on from generations was now torn to pieces. Happiness 2.0 made us start questioning traditional ways to remain happy, to spread Happiness, and to have tolerance around global knowledge of how humanity works now and over time.

Happiness 2.0, a gentle shell around the core individual Happiness, made Happiness very unique, very personal, and yet, paradoxically, very global. It did not eradicate Happiness 1.0; instead, it provided an alternative framework to obtain Happiness.

Birth of Artificial Intelligence

As these two core backbone technologies–the computer and the Internet–were getting introduced to the masses in the late 1990s, a new kind of technological advancement and source of awareness, called Artificial Intelligence, started growing slowly. It was not anticipated in the extrapolation of how technology and global human connection formed. It was a subtle start: tentative, hesitant, cautious, yet powerfully persuasive in its advance, like a baby holding the hands of the humans who gave birth to it, taking baby steps to align with the human World, learning to walk, learning to navigate.

Artificial Intelligence was conceived a bit before this century, like a zygote in the initial days when the first electronic computers came along; a tiny fledgling of a zygote, wondering whether to make a big splash of its own with a purpose to serve humans, or sit around a bit and disappear. Artificial Intelligence manifested with the invention and rapid development of computers. Before that, it was all theory.

I feel lucky to be around the right place and at the right time to see it all being put together. The IBM personal computers (P.C.) started bringing computers to the mainstream. In 1992, I saw the IBM P.C. for the first time as a student in my school's computer lab.

It was a dramatic moment for me, which I will never forget.

The computer lab was air-conditioned—the only room in the entire school. We had to remove our shoes before entering, for apparently, the dust from the shoes could penetrate the computer and make it stop working. I am not sure if that information was entirely correct. Still, we revered the computer greatly, so we respectfully complied. Somebody suggested that we wear masks and not sneeze in case the virus in our bodies got transferred to the computers. It was complete nonsense for anybody knowing anything about computers; human viruses had nothing to do with computer viruses. But even then, we complied, lest we were robbed of the Happiness of seeing this new marvel called the computer. On that fateful day, I entered the computer lab with trepidation and finally saw the fabled machine which I had only seen in pictures; the legendary C.R.T. monitor, perched atop a wide box (the CPU), where there was a floppy disk drive; connected to it, was a solitary keyboard (no mouse at that time). On the side of the box, it said "IBM".

The IBM P.C. came with the Disk Operating System (DOS) and was pre-loaded with the BASIC programming language. It was magical to type the computer code into a real computer instead of writing it on paper and simulating the logic to see the output.

As a high school student, by the time I had learned how to write code in BASIC, I could think of several creative ways to play around to create fun and exciting computer programs. I could make graphics and physics simulation-based computer games like billiards, snakes, and such, advanced for those times but trivial today in 2023.

My first tryst with Artificial Intelligence

I unknowingly took the first step into creating a basic and fledgling incarnation of our friend, Artificial Intelligence, back in 1993, when I wrote a BASIC program that could display human-sounding sentences in response to what the user typed on the screen.

At first, when I showed it to my friends, it astonished them. To their human sentences and fully formed questions as inputs, the computer responded with sentences that sounded alarmingly human-looking, with all the philosophical innuendos, albeit somewhat removed from the context of the conversation. At first, it stunned and scared them. Was this a thinking machine?

When I explained the logic of the program to my more computer-savvy friends, they realized that the smart-sounding human-like responses shown by the computer were generated dumbly by the BASIC program from an extensive list of pre-formed phrases of sentences as an extremely limited auto-complete. The choice made by the code to select a sentence phrase out of the list of terms and display it after a question from the human input followed a simple algorithm:

- If the input sentence had a word common to some of the pre-formed pre-entered phrases in the program database, the program selected one of them at random, and followed that with a random question.

- If not, the program would print out a random phrase from the list of phrases in the database and follow that again with a random question.
- The program kept track of the sentence phrases it used previously, so that sentences were not repeated.

For example, my friend typed, "How are you feeling?". The program database already had a few phrases in my prefilled list of responses that had the word "feeling", such as "I am feeling great." The word "feeling" was common to the input and as well as one of the pre-loaded phrases. Hence, the program automatically selected "I am feeling great" as a response. To make the program sound clever, the code selected another question phrase randomly from a list of questions. In this case, it chose "How is the weather today?".

So now, for my friend's question, "How are you feeling?" the computer wrote, "I am feeling great. How is the weather today?"

My friends had never seen a computer before, and to them, a machine responding like this was alarming and fanciful. It scared them and also astonished them. It sounded so real, like an actual human! Of course, after they tried out many different conversations, they realized that the computer was merely producing sentence phrases from a list it already had, followed by a random question to appear as if it wanted to have a conversation.

Although very rudimentary, my BASIC program was reasonably advanced at that time. Had I worked more on it, I would have made it more sophisticated by taking sentence phrases from encyclopedias, making the conversations more robust. It could then respond to a vast amount of conversational patterns. I would have also added some aspects of statistics so that the sentence phrases with the most statistical match with the input phrase were displayed.

My BASIC program was a hit, and unknowingly, I had stumbled upon the fundamental concept of one aspect of Artificial Intelligence 30 years back. That brings us to the question; what is Artificial Intelligence anyways? Let's take a deeper look.

What is Artificial Intelligence?

According to a typically well-accepted textbook definition, *"Artificial intelligence (A.I.) is the simulation of human intelligence processes by machines, especially computer systems."* An Artificial Intelligence system "simulates" human intelligence. It is not human. Nor does it have actual human intelligence.

By this definition, the BASIC computer program I wrote 30 years back was a (very rudimentary and bare) form of an Artificial Intelligence system. What my BASIC program did 30 years back in 1993 was close, in principle, to a modern conversational Artificial Intelligent system such as ChatGPT, Google BARD now in 2023. It simulated a real human conversation (at least, at an elementary level). It used a bit of math, probability, data, and algorithm to solve the purpose. It "appeared" intelligent to real humans, at least briefly, until they realized it was repeating itself.

An often romanticized representation of Artificial Intelligence is a kind of intelligent, non-organic, mysterious being with intelligence similar to, and even superior to, human beings. In popular cultures, the concept of humanoid robots and Artificial Intelligence are interchanged. However, a fundamental difference between a robot and an A.I. is that the former is a real object. In contrast, A.I. is an abstract set of theories and systems that appear to be intelligent systems capable of human-like responses.

A.I. needs to be manifested into interacting, tangible computer systems called A.I. agents. For example, a Roomba vacuum cleaner that moves around the room intelligently to vacuum the room, or a thermostat which turns the air conditioning on or off intelligently, or a vending machine which dispenses products, or Self-driving cars are all A.I. agents.

Smart speakers, such as Apple's Siri, Google Assistant, Amazon's Alexa, and Microsoft's Cortana are also A.I. agents. They don't have a perception of movement, yet, they have deep inbuilt A.I. systems which power them.

With the advent of systems such as ChatGPT and Google Bard, the realization of a very advanced language system that can hold a natural conversation is fast approaching. These chat systems are hyper-realistic, seem to have a "mind" of their own, and can potentially converse on any conversation patterns. Till date, these are probably the greatest manifestation of Artificial Intelligence.

A.I. and Personalization

Artificial Intelligence is also manifested in various smartphone Apps and online platforms; their presence is mainly behind the scenes and is less evident to a casual human. One of the most popular forms of it is recommender systems that one comes across in video platforms, news platforms, social media, and almost every internet forum which extracts digital content and displays them to you.

If you use Instagram, Facebook, TikTok, YouTube, LinkedIn, or any such App, you get personalized content tailored for you. These are surfaced to you using recommender systems, which likely use Artificial Intelligence to some extent.

Artificial Intelligence interacts with you indirectly through the intelligent, personalized content you see several times daily on your smartphones and other digital devices.

Our social media feeds tell us what is happening in our society; a typical social media feed algorithm has Artificial Intelligence under the hood. The news that we read on online news platforms and the videos that we endlessly, and often mindlessly, watch on TikTok, Facebook, and YouTube, are all carefully and cleverly personalized for us so that we find them engaging; the technology which does that under the hood has Artificial Intelligence driving a significant portion of it.

Targeted advertisements, personalized news and personalized content feed in our iPhones or Android devices, and the personalized search results, are all catered to us, with the intent to filter the gigantic amount of Information and awareness in this Universe to narrow it down to a few specs of Information catered just for us.

In all this magical transformation of Information and awareness in the Universe to some tiny tangible bits of Information that only we would like, Artificial Intelligence plays a significant role in **personalizing** the content for us. With personalization, you get delightfully relevant content from online platforms (**Figure 1.1**).

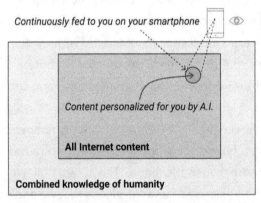

Continuously fed to you on your smartphone

Content personalized for you by A.I.

All Internet content

Combined knowledge of humanity

Figure 1.1. *Personalization of Internet content by A.I.*

Let's look at some data to understand and appreciate digital content personalization. As of 2023, around 3.7 MILLION **new** videos are uploaded to YouTube **daily**, which is approximately 271,330 hours of video content based on an average length of 4.4 minutes. If we assume there are 800 million videos on YouTube, with an average length of 11.7 minutes, it would take 9.36 billion minutes to watch it all. That's 156 million hours, 6.5 million days, or **17,810 years of consecutive video watching!** And that is just YouTube; now add TikTok, Instagram, Facebook, Vimeo, and such platforms, and imagine the amount of content.

Out of those millions of videos on just YouTube, you get a few relevant videos on the homepage and other places when you go to the YouTube homepage. From millions of videos to just a few 100 videos! How is that even possible? Let's look at how YouTube recommends personalized videos to you.

If you start "cold" at YouTube—i.e., you visit YouTube for the first time ever—you will probably see some random videos that may or may not be relevant to you. Then suppose you search for a topic of your choice, say, a song by your favorite musical artist. YouTube now shows you several videos related to that artist. You click on a few and play those songs. Soon, YouTube starts showing you other relevant videos from that Artist, similar artists, or somewhat related videos. You could click on one of them, then another, and so on. After a few interactions, YouTube sort of "figures out" what you like and starts showing you videos you will likely enjoy when you open the App every time (provided, of course, you did not explicitly ask YouTube to delete your history and forget everything about you, which it will respect). These customized collections of videos are now **personalized** for you. While it seems innocuous, under the hood, in reality, you get to see only a few directly related to you from millions of videos on YouTube.

YouTube trains machine learning models to personalize the videos for you. Machine learning is a critical tool for Artificial Intelligence. In fact, it is fair to say that Artificial Intelligence is personalizing all the content for you. After all, as per the definition, Artificial Intelligence "simulates" human intelligence. What Artificial Intelligence is doing for you on the Internet is gathering a small, personalized set of content for you and surfacing them for you at the right moment. If you had a human assistant to do it for you, they would do a similar job.

Powerful as it is, the manifestation of Artificial Intelligence through personalization could not have affected us so dramatically if smartphones had not been invented. With smartphones, we carry our friend, Artificial Intelligence, with us. Through the personalized content on our smartphones, social media, and other smartphone Apps, our view of the World, ourselves, and everything around us is subtly shaped by the personalized content shown to us by Artificial Intelligence.

Let's look at how smartphones developed and how the combination of smartphones, the Internet, and Artificial Intelligence radically changed our worldview and perception of Happiness.

Smartphones

The smartphone revolution started with the announcement of the iPhone in January 2007 by Apple CEO, Steve Jobs. Even though he helped bring smartphones to the common person, smartphones had been around before. In the 1990s, IBM introduced a device called Simon, considered the World's first smartphone. It had a touchscreen, could send and receive faxes and emails, and a calendar, address book, and calculator. The Simon was expensive, bulky, and not widely adopted. In 2000, Ericsson released the R380, the first smartphone to use the Symbian operating system. It had a color touchscreen and could access the Internet and send/receive emails. The Nokia 9210 Communicator followed soon after, featuring a full keyboard designed for business users. In 2002, BlackBerry released its first smartphone, the BlackBerry 5810, which became popular among business professionals for its secure email capabilities.

When I started my Ph.D. in Computer Science in the U.S.A. in 2003, the term "smartphone" was not popular with the masses. There were mobile phones, sure, but they were just phones. The first cool phone I had during those times was the Motorola Razr in 2004; it was cool because one had to flip it to open. It had capabilities such as taking photos, and had a screen where you could look at the text you typed.

Back then, social media had already proliferated; Orkut by Google had just started getting popular. However, we still had to have access to a computer to log into Facebook,

Orkut, Myspace, or other websites. I could not check my social media or do anything interesting on the Internet with my mobile phone. Access to social media was limited and static.

All this changed when Steve Jobs introduced the iPhone in 2007 in Silicon Valley, California. The iPhone was built on the success of its predecessors. However, it revolutionized the smartphone industry with its touchscreen, intuitive user interface, and access to the Internet. The iPhone quickly became a popular consumer device, and its App Store allowed for the creation of a vast ecosystem of third-party apps. In 2008, Google released the Android operating system, a popular alternative to Apple's iOS. Android-based smartphones quickly gained market share thanks to their affordability and flexibility.

Since then, the smartphone industry has continued to evolve rapidly. And with it came the omnipresent stream of information which led to awareness beyond one's imagination.

Omnipresent information and awareness

The advent of smartphones to the common mass population, starting in 2007, radically changed how information was presented to the user. Before smartphones, one had to find a desktop computer or a laptop with an Internet connection to look for that information on the Internet. Such computers were not only difficult to carry around but also were not generally available for mass consumption.

With the advent of the smartphone, information through the Internet became much more available on the go.

With time, as digital content providers started personalizing content tailored for the user, information became lean-out; lean-out because the Information was serendipitously presented to users without the user actively searching for it.

In 2023 now, lean-out, personalized, and serendipitously obtained digital content is available everywhere we carry our smartphones. The combined consciousness and knowledge of humanity have become a part of us, magically getting filtered by the content providers with help from our friend, Artificial Intelligence.

With such content available in a lean-out way, our awareness of things is subtly getting shaped, as is our perspective on what makes us happy. With such a lean-back and personalized awareness, the next phase of Happiness—Happiness 3.0—became a leading version of Happiness.

Happiness 3.0: personalization of Happiness

The advent of smartphones, and the lean-out personalized Internet content powered by Artificial Intelligence brought in the next generation of Happiness: **Happiness 3.0**. Happiness 3.0 is the subsequent iteration of Happiness 2.0, the fundamental difference being that Happiness 2.0 was lean-in; Happiness 3.0 is largely lean-out and personalized.

Compared to Happiness 1.0, which was limited in scope, Happiness 2.0 broke free of these limitations but still required humans to actively seek out awareness and sources of Happiness through the Internet, made available through a laptop or a desktop computer. Happiness 3.0, however, is radically different, as it is powered by Artificial Intelligence and can serendipitously provide humans with personalized awareness and content fundamentally without them having to actively seek it out.

Happiness 3.0 fundamentally differs in how it is tightly linked with the Internet, smartphones, and our friend, Artificial Intelligence. With the smartphone being an essential part of us every day, everywhere, each personalized content directly or indirectly affects Happiness 3.0.

The evolution of technology is tied to the evolution of the three versions of Happiness. In the three versions of Happiness, there is one constant: Information. Information is vital in obtaining awareness about the World, making these principles affect Happiness primarily.

How did obtaining Information change so dramatically with smartphones and Artificial Intelligence? To understand this, let's look at an important concept: the Information Horizon.

Information Horizon

Information Horizon for a person is the range of Information that a person can get from various sources. It is closely associated with the multiple dimensions by which the person is defined. Individuals are defined by their cultural association, friends, beliefs, likings, interests and hobbies, and many other sets of (sometimes) orthogonal attributes. Together, they define a person. All Information around these dimensions constitutes the *Information Horizon* for this person.

Let's look at an example to make it clear. Let me build my own Information Horizon. My Information Horizon is the limited set made out of the union of all knowledge in the Universe, which is recursively associated with my likings and associations. It is the union of all knowledge and awareness in the Universe **personalized** for me. For example, I am associated with computer technology through work. Also, I am associated with music, arts, and literature through my side passions. My Information Horizon, thus, consists of knowledge and awareness about the following:

Computer technology: My Information Horizon will have recent events in computing, different fields of computer science and engineering, famous people in computing, historical references to computing, different companies working on computer-related technologies, people associated with computer technology, and so on

Musicians, authors, and artists: My Information Horizon will also have awareness about music, arts, and literature by my favorite musicians, composers, artists, favorite authors, new trends in literature, and such. The union of all these sets of Information belongs to my Information Horizon.

Other facts related to my language and culture: My Information Horizon will also have specific knowledge and awareness about the languages I can speak and read, my culture, and such.

My Information Horizon may not contain Information not tied to me through these dimensions of computer technology, music, arts, literature, and other interests which define me. My Information Horizon, for example, may not contain Information about knowledge from the fashion industry (because I am not into that industry), nor much Information about bio-technological related Information (since I am not in that field either), and so on. Similarly, my Information Horizon will only contain Information on people and celebrities I know or follow. My Information Horizon will not have awareness about sports teams that I do not track or know about, and so on.

Information distance

Information distance between a person and a piece of information can be conceptualized as the number of different hops of information sources required for that person to learn that information, either serendipitously or through actions to seek it.

Let's look at an example: say around famous historical people. There can be several scenarios:

Low information distance: Consider famous historical people who speak a language you know, are perhaps from the same country you associate with, and whose references occur in popular culture. For me, for example, Gandhi would be such a person. The information distance between Gandhi and me is small since the mention of Gandhi occurred in our school textbooks, as well as Gandhi is in popular Indian (and global) culture. In fact, Gandhi is such a famous figure that many readers worldwide have a low information distance from Gandhi.

Large information distance: Now consider a famous historical figure from somewhere other than my country that did not occur in regular textbooks or popular culture that I am associated with, but can be somehow connected through a less-known information source. An example is the famous Japanese filmmaker and painter Akira Kurosawa. The information distance between me and Akira Kurosawa is large because I would have only heard of him if I had an interest in international movie directors of yesteryears.

Almost infinite information distance: Finally, consider a significant army war hero who played a prominent role in defending their country against external aggression. If I am from a different country or culture, and if that war hero was not mentioned in popular textbooks, chances are I will never learn about them. My information distance to this person is almost infinitely large.

Information Horizon and Happiness

Your Information Horizon plays a significant role in shaping what information gets to you, which affects your awareness and is essential in shaping your long-term Happiness.

Similar to the Happiness versions, the parallel theme of Information Horizon would be Information Horizon 1.0, 2.0, and 3.0; these are directly tied to Happiness 1.0, 2.0, and 3.0, respectively.

Information Horizon 1.0 consists of all information obtained through immediate people we interact with and from static, non-personalized information sources, such as newspapers, news channels, radio, and magazines. The information distance would be low. From our description of Happiness 1.0, Information Horizon 1.0 is directly linked to Happiness 1.0.

Information Horizon 2.0 consists of all information from Information 1.0 PLUS information from Internet searches. By definition, the information distance of this kind of Information is relatively high, but due to the Internet, we can find those eventually, provided we know what to search for. Information 2.0 allows us to explore various topics and learn quickly. This can be a recursive process, as we may find one topic leads to another and then another. Information Horizon 2.0 is directly linked to Happiness 2.0.

Information Horizon 3.0 consists of all information from Information Horizon 2.0 PLUS what we get from personalization digital content surfacing through Internet platforms. Due to its source of personalized information, it is closely linked with personalized Artificial Intelligence (A.I.). The reach of Information 3.0 is even broader than Information Horizon 2.0. Information with a vast information distance can still reach us through targeted and personalized digital content through social media feeds, personalized news, customized ads, and so on.

Awareness, Information Horizon 3.0, and Happiness 3.0

Happiness 3.0's uniqueness comes from the combination of three prominent technologies—the Internet, Artificial Intelligence, and smartphones—which have made our Information Horizon vast. Happiness 3.0 is a derivative of the immense Information Horizon 3.0 that Artificial Intelligence and digital Technologies opened to us. The vastness of Information Horizon 3.0 significantly influences our perception of the World around us, most of the time subconsciously without putting direct effort into it.

I can bring my own example here to demonstrate how the effect of a vast Information Horizon 3.0 directly affects my worldview. I have watched several television series and movies on Netflix. They are from various languages and cultures that I was not aware of, as well as languages and cultures that I grew up around. I did not actively look for them. So we can say these movies are at a very large Information distance from me. Yet, they were recommended to me by Netflix algorithms, which employ machine learning (a key component in Artificial Intelligence, as we discussed above) to surface personalized recommendations. I would have never watched these movies had they not been recommended by Netflix, mainly because they are at a significant information distance from me. I do not know these languages and depend entirely on English subtitles, yet the content appeals to me.

The Netflix algorithms, powered by Artificial Intelligence under the hood, cleverly surfaced these contents, personalized to my taste and liking. Watching these movies has changed my world viewpoint. I have become a great fan of these contents, the finesse displayed in the art of storytelling, the cultural values, the food, the people, and the place. My worldview about these new cultures has changed for good, and I am waiting for a chance to visit these places in person as a tourist and seep it all in.

The same happens for music; I got introduced to a wide range of music through YouTube music and Spotify; they are now a consistent part of my music playlist, along with content from all over the World.

The intense personalization of content which makes me happy to engage with could be possible due to the intelligent algorithms employing some form of Artificial Intelligence. These new music recommendations by YouTube music dramatically expand my worldview on different forms of music dramatically. The same goes for YouTube and its chain of recommended videos recursively showing endless videos; each ingested video leaves some impression on me, positive or, at times, negative. Similarly, many news channels are personalized; each time personalized news reaches me, I learn about some global event or a local social event, even if I have yet to seek out to actively look for it. That, again, influences my worldview.

Besides entertainment, social media feeds on Instagram, Facebook, and LinkedIn give me new insights and reference data for constantly renewing my worldview. This especially happens due to serendipitous suggestions by social media platforms to subscribe to groups, ranging from groups that follow famous people to groups that discuss abstract concepts. The group suggestions in social media are personalized, customized, and recommended for me out of thousands. Each of these groups, with its diverse set of people from all over the World sharing their opinions, helps me constantly shape my worldview. This happens to me, and I am sure it has happened to many of us on social media. This is all possible due to the intense personalization that these social media feeds do, with Artificial Intelligence under the hood.

With ever-evolving world views powered by Artificial Intelligence and its effect on Information Horizon 3.0, the intensely personalized Happiness 3.0 also gets affected and re-shaped. New things affect Happiness with each new change in worldview. A new place. A new culture. A new series of entertainment. A newly discovered artist, musician, or entertainer.

The World is buzzing with billions of content and artifacts which can bring Happiness. Through digitization and personalization, our Information Horizon 3.0 is so vast that even these Billions of content, with enormous information distances, are customized and presented to us.

The Merging of Artificial Intelligence with Human Happiness

Through Information Horizon 3.0, Artificial Intelligence has merged with human Happiness, giving us the new version, Happiness 3.0. In 2023 now, every time we log into some smartphone App that surfaces personalized content for us, we get somehow tied with it, and eventually to the immense influence of Artificial Intelligence which is powering many of these apps.

The key metric Artificial Intelligence optimizes through all these Apps is engagement, essentially making us increasingly engaged with the content surfaced from the App. That's why you get hooked onto these Apps, be it Instagram, Facebook, YouTube, TikTok, or any other such App. One key aspect is that Happiness is not the key metric optimized in these Apps. Engagement is. Whether the engagement makes us happy or not is something we will talk about for the rest of the book. But this form of Happiness, Happiness 3.0, is here to stay forever, as long as you use any Internet technology and do not disconnect yourself entirely from the Internet.

It looks like Happiness 1.0 transitioned into Happiness 3.0 in less than a decade. The first transition to Happiness 2.0 happened when a common person could use the Internet in 1997 to escape the immediate influence of human connections for Information. It changed within a decade when the Internet became omnipresent with the smartphone. All the World's Information to directly influence Happiness came to the forefront in the smartphone, omnipresent and unavoidable, to transform Happiness 2.0 into Happiness 3.0.

Yet, it cannot be truly called a transition. The latest versions of Happiness only partially take over the older versions. Instead, all three versions coexist and may even intersect in their basic premises. Each one of us, though, mixes the three versions very differently; it is very personal, very time and context-dependent.

For example, I mix the three versions of Happiness throughout the day, every day. When I interact with my friends, family, and colleagues, it's all personal, direct contact, and Happiness 1.0 is in full effect. At other times, I seek out information related to my work or any other aspect, and Happiness 2.0 kicks in. And then, there are times when I carelessly check my smartphone and social media where I get shown targeted, personalized content which may directly affect my worldview and Happiness, which makes me plunge into Happiness 3.0.

All versions of Happiness coexist. Yet, Happiness 3.0 is the new, primarily dominant version of Happiness over all others. That is because this version encompasses all the aspects of its previous versions. There is something in how we are tied with smartphones and personalized digital content permanently and continually every day, which makes us prone to make Happiness 3.0 the primary version of Happiness.

And through Happiness 3.0, we have quietly invited our friend, Artificial Intelligence, to control us and our lives by subtly dictating what we should think about, what we should like, what we should do next, whom to like, and how to like.

Our friend, Artificial Intelligence, has been evolving subtly under the hood of Internet and mobile technologies. With its advance, we humans are slowly getting entangled with it in a way that directly contributes to our Happiness 3.0. And now, in 2023, we are so entangled with Artificial Intelligence that it subtly affects the fundamental way we live our lives. Now that A.I. is omnipresent in almost all technology we interact with, Happiness 3.0 now coexists with Happiness 1.0 and 2.0 permanently. Unless you stay in a cave, completely isolated from the Internet, there is no looking back.

Is this friend of ours, A.I., something wonderfully delightful and benign? Or, lurking along its friendliness, does there lie another startling dimension slowly gripping humanity in an unescapable bondage from which we can never free ourselves? Should we be adapting to the fact that our daily Happiness is subtly controlled by A.I.? Did the unintended consequence of A.I. shaping Happiness 1.0 into Happiness 3.0 makes us depend too much on this friend? Should we be adopting this omnipresent A.I. and the effect it has on Happiness 3.0 at large?

Or, instead of being alarmist and fearful over what A.I. can do, should we instead harness the extraordinary power of our friend, A.I., to optimize and sustain Happiness 3.0? And if we do, is there a way to quantify and measure Happiness so that we can then make a case of whether A.I. is increasing, or diminishing it, with the ultimate goal of optimizing Happiness 3.0?

If so, how do we measure Happiness, model it, or optimize it? How does A.I. affect all this?

Let's find out in the following chapters.

CHAPTER 2

Properties of Happiness

Before attempting to model and optimize Happiness 3.0, we will first derive some properties of Happiness in this Chapter. We will discuss some simple foundations which will enable us to look at Happiness more objectively than being a metaphorical state of mind. I will borrow from observations that govern this Universe and use those principles to understand the state of Happiness.

Building these foundational premises is useful to objectively look at Happiness. These premises are essential for us to finally embark on the fundamental question: how can we model and optimize Happiness 3.0? That will be discussed in great depth in the next chapter, where I will present a model of Happiness and then proceed to talk about the model objectively built upon the basic principles and structures developed in this chapter.

Measuring Happiness

It's tempting to put some structure around measuring Happiness quantitatively so that we can look at it more structurally. The Merriam-Webster dictionary defines Happiness as "a state of well-being and contentment." So Happiness is a state. And a state is most often measurable.

Let's consider two (hypothetical) people, John and Mary. The most straightforward measurement or quantification of Happiness is a Boolean function that returns a true or false. We can quantify John and Mary's Happiness in the last 6 months as

happiness(Mary, 6 months) = true
happiness(John, 6 months) = false

The above equation implies that Mary was happy in the previous six months and John was not.

Although this representation works, it oversimplifies the measurement. Does it mean that Mary was happy all the time in the last six months, or was John unhappy all the time in the previous six months?

An improved measurement of Happiness is one whose range value is a number instead of a Boolean true or false. The improved measurement would return a number between 0 and 1, giving a reasonable estimate of X's Happiness in interval T. For example:

happiness(Mary, 6 months) = 0.8
happiness(John, 6 months) = 0.7

The above means that Mary was happy 80% of the time in the past six months, and John was happy 70%.

This improved function value has some fundamental advantages: it gives a more realistic measurement, is comparable, and is normalized. For example, we can now observe that Mary was happier than John on average in the last six months.

A pragmatic way to estimate the value of this function would be to ask Mary and John to keep a journal every day for six months and jot down the occasions that made them happy and those that made them unhappy. Say Mary journals h instances of being happy, and u instances of being unhappy or neutral in her 6-month Happiness journal. Then a simplistic Happiness measurement for Mary would be:

$$\text{happiness(Mary, 6 months)} = \frac{h}{h + u}$$

The above formula is simple enough and requires no deep knowledge or understanding of Mathematics. It calculates a simple ratio of the instances that Mary was happy out of all the cases of happy and unhappy or neutral journal entries.

We can improve the function further by adding a way to represent context. For example, even though Mary was happier than John on an average in the last 6 months, maybe just in the context of her career, she was less so. We can add a way to represent the context in the function as a suffix to the function:

$$\text{happiness}_{Career}(\text{Mary, 6 months}) <$$
$$\text{happiness}_{Career}(\text{John, 6 Months})$$

This representation gives us a powerful way of looking at various aspects of Happiness. For the more mathematically oriented reader, note that, simple as the function seems, it is essentially a probability distribution, which gives us a profound range of possibilities to play around with it to come up with delightful observations and analyses. But we will save that for the reader to play around with. For now, let us just use this simple measurement of Happiness.

Now, having defined an objective way of measuring and comparing Happiness, let's look at some properties of Happiness.

Is Happiness Absolute or Relative?

Albert Einstein, arguably one of the most significant theoretical physicists of all time, met the Indian poet, composer, thinker and towering literary figure Rabindranath Tagore a few times in the 1920s and early 1930s. By then, both men had reached international fame in their respective fields; Einstein had won the Nobel Prize for Physics in 1922, and Tagore had won the Nobel Prize for Literature in 1913.

In one of their much-celebrated discussions in Berlin in 1930, Tagore, the poet, asked Einstein, the physicist: "What is the nature of truth?" Einstein said that truth was independent of human beings. Tagore countered that truth, one with the universal being, must be essentially human;

otherwise, whatever we individuals realize as true, can never be called truth. At least, the truth is described as scientific and can only be reached through logic—in other words, by a human organ of thought. Einstein said a table in a house would remain in the room irrespective of the observer. Tagore said a table in a room made no sense if there was nobody there to call the table a table.

These two great thinkers discussed the nature of truth, a fundamental jargon that still needs an answer. In the special theory of relativity, Einstein revealed that observers in relative motion experience time differently: two events can happen simultaneously from the perspective of one observer yet happen at different times from the perspective of the other. And both observers would be correct. Does this agree with what Tagore was talking about truth being relative?

However, Einstein also said that irrespective of the frame of reference, the speed of light will remain the same from both measurements. Maybe Einstein's belief that truth is absolute has some bearing on this observation?

Absolute and relative. These two contrasting explanations of the same state have been the topic of much discussion amongst physicists, philosophers, astronomers, and thinkers, around the planet, across centuries of evolution of the human understanding of the world around them.

In a similar analogy, is Happiness absolute, or is it relative?

Happiness is, for all practical purposes, considered *relative*. Relativity of Happiness can be across different aspects.

For example, Happiness can vary from person to person and be influenced by individual circumstances, perspectives, and comparisons. Different people have different criteria for what brings them happiness, and what may make one person happy could have a different effect on another. People's happiness can be affected by their social and cultural contexts, as well as their expectations and aspirations. Happiness, being subjective, can differ significantly from one person to another.

Let's demonstrate this with a simple example. An underprivileged child can be understandably unhappier than a privileged child. Yet, a simple event, such as getting a meal, can make the underprivileged child very happy, whereas it can be a mundane and regular event for a privileged child. In terms of Happiness measurement, we can say:

$$happiness_{Gets\ a\ meal}(underprivileged\ child) >$$
$$happiness_{Gets\ a\ meal}(privileged\ child)$$

Happiness can also be relative within a single person. For example, what made you happy six months back might not make you happy anymore. This can be explained using "Hedonistic Adaptation".

Hedonistic Adaptation

Hedonistic adaptation refers to the psychological phenomenon where individuals return to their baseline level of Happiness or subjective well-being after experiencing positive or negative life events or changes. According to this concept, no matter what positive or negative events occur in a person's life, their overall level of Happiness tends to stabilize and revert to a set point.

For example, suppose John receives a significant promotion and experiences an increase in income. In that case, John may initially feel a surge of Happiness and improved life satisfaction. However, John adapts to the new circumstance over time, say six months. The increased income becomes normal. As a result, John's level of Happiness may return to the previous baseline, and they may start desiring even higher levels of income or material success to experience the same level of Happiness again. **Figure 2.1** demonstrates this.

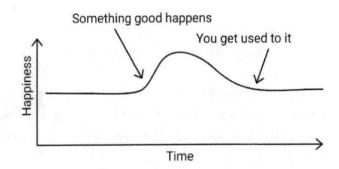

Figure 2.1. Hedonistic Adaptation

In terms of happiness measurement equation, it can be expressed as:

$$happiness_{Promoted}(John, present\ time) <$$
$$happiness_{Promoted}(John, 6\ months\ back)$$

Perspective

Whether an event makes a person happy or not can depend on the perspective.

Take the example of a sports match: the 2022 soccer world cup final between Argentina and France. It was a closely contested match between two fantastic teams, each with two personal greats; Lionel Messi (Argentina) and Kylian Mbappe (France).

Suppose there is a neutral person who is not invested in soccer but is nevertheless interested in knowing what happened there. The point of view of the match will be completely different based on who is describing the match.

The Argentina fans of the winning team will probably rave about what their best players did in the match or turning points in the match.

The France team fans would talk about a different perspective and point to turning points or unfortunate turns in the game, which made them eventually lose the match despite putting up a tremendous fight.

The fans of the Argentina team would be having a wild celebration worldwide after winning the world cup, and the

France team fans would probably be more unhappy and rue on missed chances.

To cap it in terms of perspective and Happiness, the Argentina team fans were happy; the France team fans were less. At that moment, other considerations, such as wealth, connections, or other factors, were downplayed. The fact that their favorite team won or lost played a significant role in determining the Happiness of the two fans, who had different perspectives depending on whose side of the game they were in. So:

$$happiness_{World\ Cup\ Final}(Argentina\ team\ fan) >$$
$$happiness_{World\ Cup\ Final}(France\ team\ fan)$$

In all these discussions, we can draw one parallel: that Happiness too depends on the perspective of who the observer is, what the occasion is, on which side of the event one is, and a variety of factors beyond one's choosing. The same event can provoke feelings of Happiness, sadness, or neutral reactions, to other people witnessing or being involved in the event.

Rashomon Effect

Varying perspectives affecting Happiness differently for different people for the same event can be explained through the Rashomon effect. The Rashomon effect is a storytelling and writing method in cinema in which the individuals involved give an event contradictory interpretations or descriptions, thereby providing different perspectives and points of view of the same incident. The Rashomon effect is named after the film Rashomon, a 1950 Japanese psychological thriller-crime film written and directed by the famed movie director Akira Kurosawa. The film was given an Academy Honorary Award at the 24th Academy Awards in 1952 and is considered one of the greatest films ever made.

Akin to the Rashomon effect, Happiness depends on the individual's perspective.

An analogy to explain this is the story of blind people in a room with an elephant. The parable of the blind men and an Elephant is a story of a group of blind men who have never encountered an elephant before and who learn and imagine what the elephant is like by touching it. Each blind man feels a different part of the elephant's body, but only one part, such as the side or the tusk. They then describe the elephant based on their limited experience, and their descriptions of the elephant differ. The one touching the tail says that the elephant is like a rope; the one touching the trunk says the elephant is like a snake; the one touching the side says the elephant is like a wall, and so on.

We can look at another example borrowing from Geometry: changing perspective is akin to rotating an object around an axis so that the viewpoint is different. Take a cylinder as an example. It looks like a rectangle if you look at it from the side and remove all the shades. Tilt it a bit, and your mind figures out it is a cylinder. Look at it from the bottom: it appears to be a circle.

Entanglement

We have built the objective properties of Happiness with the principle that Happiness of a person depends on circumstances that they face. However, we are part of a large fabric of the Universe, and events happening to another person might affect our Happiness.

To model this property of Happiness with a corresponding property of the Universe, let's look at a relevant and startling Physics concept called *quantum entanglement*. Quantum entanglement is an invisible (and undefined) link between distant quantum objects that allows one to affect the other instantly.

Einstein predicted it, albeit in a 1935 paper, he argued that his quantum theory was illogically pointing out the entanglement as, 'Measurement of one particle could instantaneously affect the measurement of another particle, no matter the distance of separation between them.' Yet, years later, this strange phenomenon, predicted by Einstein, started getting to be proved in labs around the world.

The research for years on quantum entanglement culminated in 2022, when Alain Aspect, John Clauser, and Anton Zeilinger won the Nobel Prize in physics for experiments with entangled photons. The three researchers conducted experiments that showed a unique state called "entanglement," when multiple tiny particles are linked, in a sense, so that what happens to one determines what happens to the others, even when large distances separate them. When a scientist determines the state of a particle, all the others that are "entangled" with it will immediately take on the same state, regardless of where they are, even if they're in a distant galaxy.

What has entanglement to do with our measurement of Happiness? We can create an analogy: when two persons are 'entangled' in any abstract way, the change in state in one affects that of the other. This can happen even if they are at a large interaction distance from each other; i.e. they may not even know each other, nor have any relationship, yet, they can be entangled. It can also occur if these persons are not related to each other in any tangible way.

For example, entanglement is seen every time you drive. When you drive, you assume that the other drivers in your vicinity drive correctly. If they don't, you can get into a crash. You are thus 'entangled' with the other drivers in your vicinity; a change in the state of one of the drivers—maybe a wrong turn or a sudden brake—can affect your driving and safety.

In our example above, if Mary is entangled with John, it is likely that Mary's Happiness, when entangled with John, is different from that of her independent Happiness. For example, Mary likes John (a relatively straightforward and measurable form of entanglement). As a result, if she learns about John's state that makes him unhappy, her Happiness ebbs away somewhat; the equation then becomes

$$happiness_{\text{Entangled with John}}(Mary) <$$
$$happiness_{\text{not entangled with John}}(Mary)$$

Is the amount of Happiness constant in the Universe?

So far we see that Happiness is relative, depends on perspective, and can be affected by events happening to somebody else who is entangled to you. One key question that needs to be discussed now is: is there a limit to the amount of Happiness in this Universe?

Let's model Happiness as energy in this context. The conservation of energy is a fundamental principle in physics, stating that energy cannot be created or destroyed; it can only be transferred or transformed into another form. According to the law of conservation of energy, the total energy of an isolated system, which is not influenced by external forces, remains constant. This concept is derived from the first law of thermodynamics, also known as the law of energy conservation.

As an example, a ball dropped from a height gains kinetic energy due to its motion. At the same time, it loses an equal amount of potential energy because it is moving closer to the ground. When the ball reaches the ground, its initial potential energy gets converted into kinetic energy. The total energy is conserved throughout the process; only it gets redistributed.

A compelling parallel argument is: Happiness, too, remains constant; it can be redistributed between different groups of people and individuals depending on the outcome of events, especially in a closed event.

Let's draw some parallels. Consider the soccer game from the above example again. As the game is about to begin, the fans on both sides have equal hope that their side might win. After the game, the fans of the losing side are arguably unhappy, while those of the winning side are happy. The initial amount of Happiness reserved for the game (a closed system) is now transferred to the fans of the winning side. It is limited and gets massively skewed.

Another example: look at one's career. Promotions and growth are always competitive; you might miss your promotion due to somebody else getting ahead of you, or vice versa. Assuming that the one getting promoted is happy and the one being denied is unhappy, the limited Happiness associated with promotion gets distributed unevenly.

Competition makes Happiness limited

From the examples above, Happiness seems to be limited because of the inherent competitive nature of humans. All competitions are built around the principle that there is a winning side and a losing side. It can be predicted reasonably accurately that the winning side is (at least temporarily) happier than the losing side. The 'amount' of

Happiness is limited; it gets distributed to the winning side, who gets the favorable outcome of the event which provides Happiness.

The argument of limited Happiness in the entirety of humanity is even starker when compared to the distribution of wealth (we will talk more about it in detail in the next chapter). If Happiness is correlated with wealth, can it be distributed likewise, too? Can we say that roughly 80% of the world's wealth/Happiness is distributed to 20% of individuals? We will discuss more about this in the next chapter.

Take, for example, the real estate pricing in Silicon Valley. As of 2023, a median Silicon Valley home will cost anybody around 1.4 million US dollars. Naturally, high earners get plum homes (and the Happiness associated with having a desirable home to stay in); others who cannot afford that price are relegated to homes they might not like that much, but be forced to consider.

Happiness, thus, seems limited in quantity; it will get distributed unevenly to people who can afford it (literally) and disfavor those who cannot afford it. (The next chapter will delve deeper into the relationship between wealth and Happiness). This comes down to competition; the one ahead in terms of acquiring wealth gets the plum homes and the Happiness associated with it.

The history of humanity is riddled with uneven distribution of limited availability of Happiness. Before the system of governments and common laws set in most countries, the system of having a ruler of the country, and other "commoners" who served the king, was the system.

The rulers had most of the wealth, most of the power to influence anything that could bring Happiness, and astronomically more power to decide their fates and gather all resources to maximize Happiness.

The "commoners" were mostly distant from these aspirations; history is full of examples of the "commoners" living an unhappy life at large, devoid of resources of Happiness even at a basic level. At the same time, the rulers had a disproportionate amount of resources available to make them happy for generations.

The argument seems to hold that Happiness is of "a limited quantity" and sort of constant, akin to energy being constant in a closed system.

Is Happiness Utopia possible?

Given that Happiness is limited, is it possible to attain that perfect state in the Universe where everybody is happy? This would mean that the limited Happiness is distributed equitably to everybody.

I often recall John Lennon's eternally beautiful song "Imagine." John Lennon's song "Imagine" is an influential and iconic anthem that promotes unity, peace, and a world free from divisions. Its lyrics envision a world without borders, religions, or material possessions, where people live harmoniously and embrace a shared humanity. It encourages listeners to imagine a better world. It inspires them to work towards creating a more peaceful and inclusive society.

In such a Utopian world "imagined" by John Lennon, the limited quality of Happiness would be more evenly distributed. Embracing a shared humanity seems like an ideal world.

The concept, although excellent, will likely continue to be a fantasy because it seems humans are programmed to be competitive, as I discussed in the first chapter. Given our premise of Happiness being in limited quantity in this Universe, and from the examples I mentioned just a while back, competition will automatically skew Happiness, whether we like it or not or whether that was an intention.

Let's give this some more thought. In John Lennon's song, the hypothetical world would not need any competition (so to speak).

What would such a world look like?

No borders would mean people do not fight for their country's identity of resources. No religion means there would be no religion-based tensions and hatred.

There would be no divisions based on other factors such as wealth too.

This is an aspect where the problem starts.

Would that mean that every human on the planet would live in the same size home and have the same (or similar) wealth to buy things that would sustain their livelihood and make them happy? Would there be no competition when it comes to promotions, growth, and career progression—

everybody gets to grow at the same speed, irrespective of whether they are capable or not?

In such a world, would everybody earn the same regardless of their talents? Would everybody get the same irrespective of one person being more equipped in discipline and hard work to get those things? Would a person who has no desire to do much good to the world, or contribute anything substantially to this world, have the same resources to thrive in this world as another person who is much better at their work, contributes significantly to the world, and has more capability to progress in life?

The question now becomes: what does living in harmony, with no boundaries, and having the same share of Happiness and resources mean anyways?

Looking at the Utopian world with a closer lens brings the fundamental observation up close: human beings are starkly different from each other, and it seems the nature of humans to compete with each other makes Happiness unevenly distributed. Whether that competition is fair, unfair, or favored to a specific set of parties is a different argument we will not dwell on in this book. But obtaining John Lennon's Utopian world is challenging to create due to the limited amount of Happiness, and the competitive nature of humans to get more than others.

The How of Happiness

Given that Happiness is limited in supply, it is useful to be aware of aspects of Happiness which are in our control.

Almost a quarter into the twenty-first century, a cumulation of research, wisdom, and thought experiments has revealed a very high-level generic disposition of Happiness. In 2008, American professor Sonja Lyubomirsky published a book, "The How of Happiness." The premise of "The How of Happiness" is that 50 percent of a given human's long-term Happiness level is genetically determined, 10 percent is affected by life circumstances and situations, and 40 percent of Happiness is subject to self-control through intentional activities.

Looking back at the CEO and the gardener from my childhood story, this distribution of the "hows" of Happiness might throw some interesting light. How do the 40% attribution to self-control and intentional activities affect the CEO and the gardener?

From a modern perspective, assuming that the gardener does not hold any secrets of wealth or responsibilities, he is utilizing this 40% for immediate Happiness but not optimizing for the long term by being laid back and lazy during the present time and not investing in the future.

The CEO is sacrificing a little bit of short-term Happiness but building the foundation for sustained Happiness for the longer term. It can be predicted that the gardener, with his lazy attitude towards work and growth, will eventually need more wealth or other resources required for sustained Happiness. In contrast, the CEO will have greater wealth, purpose, and achievements and empower his family and others around him to follow their own paths of Happiness.

Short-term vs. long-term Happiness

The different methods employed by the CEO and the gardener brings us to another interesting property of Happiness: *short-term* vs *long-term*. Will sacrificing Happiness for the short term, with a vision to prolong and sustain it for the long time, be a better alternative, as the CEO did? Or is focusing on short-term immediate Happiness, but not bothering too much about the longer-term sustainability of Happiness, a better option, like what the gardener was trying to do? Or, even better, is there a third option—an ideal option—where a person optimizes for both short-term and long-term Happiness?

Most cultures worldwide, throughout the history of humankind, have pursued the first option: sacrifice a bit in the short term to build long-term Happiness.

There can be exceptions to this theory, but at large, the general wisdom that has prevailed for most people is around initially building physical/abstract/intellectual wealth, making bets for the future, with the hope that eventually, there will be a tranquil state of Happiness that will sustain throughout life. It has been the classic method to obtain Happiness; the process has been perfected and optimized over centuries of wisdom passed on from generations.

Not optimized for Happiness

The trajectory of Happiness seems to be set on norms and expectations. We seldom question these norms. It starts at an early age, when children aged five (or six) are put into school. School mandates the youngsters to come in at least five days a week, for several hours daily, to inherit knowledge (whether they want to or not), be taught (or sometimes forced?) ideas and notions around how the world operates, taught math, language, geography, (perhaps somewhat distorted) history, and other subjects.

In all these established norms of education, the metric to optimize has always been the amount of knowledge, and to inculcate the nature of competition from an early age so that they can thrive in the future. That has been the system for ages. It is the established norm.

Instead, perhaps there could be alternate ways of imparting education which cater to the children's Happiness as the metric to optimize. However, that does not seem plausible. Happiness is supposed to be sustained and obtained through pain and learning and non-ideal routines of more work and less play. There are several aspects of schooling which are directly cause of unhappiness:

Schools starting way too early: I am still unclear why schools for children start in weary mornings; almost every child I have interacted with complains about waking up early, almost groggy and tired, to do their morning routines to rush to school. Who set this norm? Why give huge loads of homework, which the child has to do till night, and ask them to wake early again the next day?

Hours and hours of education: Why are children made to go through hours and hours of school? To learn, and learn some more? Is there a better way to prepare them for life, and at the same time, optimize their happiness for the journey of education instead of always preparing for the destination?

Often irrelevant education: Why are children taught a wide range of seemingly irrelevant information in schools? What is the purpose? Each child has certain strengths; why are they tested on subjects they are not strong at, and subsequently, get discouraged when they do not perform well?

I do not have a clear answer to the above questions. I am sure there are established, well-researched methods obtained through years of adjustment and optimization, resulting in today's education system. I am not an expert on this, but from my experience, I can summarize that optimizing children's Happiness was not the critical factor in deciding educational norms across the planet.

A journey vs a destination

From the plight of children mentioned above, it seems Happiness has been predefined and "optimized" through "wisdom" passed on from generations, imposed as long-term investments in education through schooling. Once a person is done through high school, youngsters are expected to seek a way to either continue education with the final outcome to obtain a livelihood or, in some cases, take on means of livelihood.

Each individual is supposed to be purpose-driven to contribute to their immediate family or to themselves, to have the basics like food, shelter, clothing, and other means of living. Of course, there are exceptions: extreme wealth, or in situations where one does not have to worry about working to get a living, or in the extreme end, abject poverty, where people just give up on trying to live and scrap by. But at large, the common wisdom is to attend schools, get knowledge, get a job, earn money, have a family, grow old, and retire.

In the grand theme of living, Happiness is not generally meant to be a **journey**; rather it is meant to be a **destination**. More involved people try to make it a journey by extracting reason and purpose to live through every day. For the majority, though, it seems Happiness takes a back seat; going through life, in whatever stages of life they are in, seems to be the norm.

Happiness is supposed to be held back at present, to some extent, so that it can increase or sustain, in the future and eventually level out and optimize over time. Do so and so, and you will end up happy. There are extremes, as we saw above, but overall, for most of humankind, the equation of school to work to family to retirement is a general theme of destination for Happiness in the longer term. In other words, a greedy approach to obtaining immediate Happiness and not thinking of longer-term preparation to be happy has been frowned upon.

Optimize for Happiness

We talked about children being made to go to school daily on weekdays for education. They grow up to earn money for themselves, and more so often, for their families, until the World decides that they are to retire. Old age catches up, and eventually, they leave this world, having gone through the cycle of life and death.

The big question remains: what percentage of the time did these people, in their cycle of birth, to childhood, to adolescence, to middle age, and then finally old age, try to optimize for Happiness instead of optimizing the means to live?

Is living the same as being happy?

Is optimizing for a life set by expectations the same as optimizing for Happiness?

It seems we have a lot of questions, but norms and expectations from life have tamed us into not asking these questions, but rather accepting them and moving on.

Do social norms and expectations constrict us so much that we end up sacrificing our Happiness to justify some "expected" social behavior, which seems to favor making Happiness a destination rather than a journey? I have seen anecdotal evidence that this holds true for several aspects.

In several cultures, academic excellence as a student holds supreme merit, as opposed to merit in other disciplines. As a child, in such cultures, if you do well in academia, it supersedes everything else. The other side is equally valid: if the child is not good at academia, there is a general sense of anxiety and disappointment seen in parents.

Being of South Asian descent myself, I can see this quite prevalent in my culture. This is not limited to childhood; even in adulthood, the title of the job has equal importance, if not more, than job satisfaction and aptitude. Parents, from an early age, encourage their children to pursue some STEM fields (Science, Technology, Engineering, and Mathematics), or perhaps to become a doctor or a lawyer, as opposed to pursuing other non-traditional disciplines such as music, arts, or such. Of course, there is a possible economic reason for this: academic achievements correlate with higher educational attainment, which in turn, correlates with better jobs and prospects of earning potential.

This culture has its own great benefits, except for students and people who are "forced" to follow a career (and often, life) path which they do not enjoy; a path which does not make them happy. Happiness at the moment, it seems, is not important in these scenarios. Going by our previous discussions, the destination becomes more important than the journey.

To put more structure around computing Happiness, based on observations of how an ideal Happiness measurement would function so far, let's first define a sensible, measurable method to compute Happiness numerically through common wisdom. I would like to call it the **Happiness formula**.

The Happiness Formula

We can define a simple formula to calculate Happiness numerically as follows:

$$\text{happiness} = \frac{What\ you\ have}{What\ you\ desire}$$

This simple equation, called the *Happiness formula*, is tremendously insightful. If one's desires stay in sync with what they have, Happiness remains consistent. If the desire goes up, but what one has remains the same, Happiness decreases. If desire lessens, and what one has remains constant, Happiness increases.

The Happiness formula can be applied to various situations; small and big, and to all kinds of people and situations.

Let's look at an innocuous example: you have some food in your refrigerator but desire something else. It's past midnight, and all shops are closed. You cannot have the food you want. Your desire (denominator) is more than what you have (numerator). You are (momentarily) unhappy.

Another example: you are very busy, and you have less time (numerator). You want more time to spend time doing things you love (denominator). The Happiness formula returns a low Happiness score.

These examples seem to point to minimalism as a life choice. Keep 'what you desire' minimal, and then Happiness will increase. If the desire is minimal, then 'having' small things makes one happier, and at least, makes Happiness more balanced and consistently sustained.

Minimalism is a lifestyle or design aesthetic focusing on simplicity, functionality, and eliminating excess. It is about reducing clutter, streamlining possessions, and prioritizing what is truly essential. Minimalism can be applied to various aspects of life, including physical possessions, relationships, work, and even digital presence. In terms of material possessions, minimalism encourages owning and keeping only necessary items or bringing joy, while eliminating unnecessary clutter. This approach emphasizes quality over quantity and promotes more intentional and mindful consumption.

In reality, living a minimalist life is difficult. In all its simplicity, most people fail to keep the denominator (what one desires) in check. As desire increases, Happiness decreases, unless the numerator similarly increases (what you have).

(More on this later; I have dedicated an entire chapter (next chapter) to modeling Happiness and mulling on optimization.)

The value returned by the Happiness formula has several excellent properties:

Comparable: It conforms to all the observations about comparing Happiness made so far. That is because the Happiness formula returns a number, and thus, makes it possible to compare Happiness between say John and Mary objectively instead of subjectively or philosophically.

Optimizable: Having a numeric value means we can look at some pragmatic methods to optimize the Happiness formula, by mapping it to philosophical ways of becoming happy, learned through generations of wisdom.

Conforms to observations: It behaves in a way we expect people's Happiness to behave; as in, Happiness can go up or down over time, context, circumstance, and all that. (For the more astute reader, the Happiness measurements mentioned above assumed that Happiness measurement was normalized; that is, it takes a value between [0, 1]. For the sake of simplicity, we assume that the Happiness formula returns a value from [0,1] through some kind of a normalization function not shown here).

What really makes us happy?

Having derived some properties of Happiness, some immediate follow-up questions arise: what can go to the numerator and the denominator of the Happiness formula? What are the aspects which make this formula stable over time?

It is intriguing to come up with a tangible Happiness model which can help us obtain and sustain Happiness more systematically. Let us look at a model of Happiness in the next chapter, and ways to optimize them.

CHAPTER 3

Modelling Happiness

A tree model of Happiness

What makes a person happy? Or rather, a slight precursor to this problem can be: what factors go into determining somebody's Happiness? **Figure 3.1** shows a classic Happiness model pertinent today in the twenty-first century. Wealth, health, freedom, purpose, and inner peace can be balanced wisely to attain an ideal state.

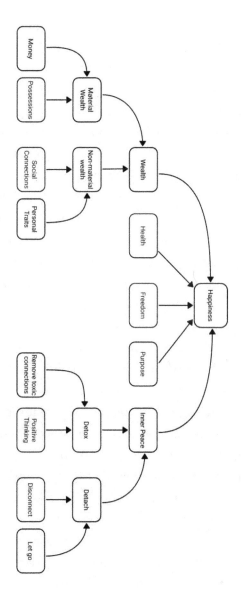

Figure 3.1. Happiness Tree

Let's start with the most important factor directly affecting Happiness: inner peace.

Inner peace

Inner peace is a state of tranquility, contentment, and harmony within oneself: a deep sense of calmness and emotional well-being arising from accepting oneself, managing stress, and finding balance.

The gardener from my childhood story achieved inner peace, as apparent from his lifestyle and attitude toward life. As a child, I didn't quite understand what inner peace meant, nor did I dwell on it. Now, years after hearing that story, I realize that the interpretation of the gardener's simple lifestyle and laidback attitude implied a deep inner peace that he had within himself.

He seemed to have figured out life!

It did not matter whether he procrastinated, did not seem to have a greater goal or purpose, or did not care to think of improving his lifestyle; his being satisfied with his daily state appeared to imply inner peace. There may be more optimal or recommended ways of leading a life. Still, he figured out how to attain that inner peace where the external factors, growth expectations, and the perpetual noise from the World did not perturb him.

Obtaining inner peace is an internal quality. It depends substantially on one's reaction to external stimuli. Understandably, retaining inner peace for physically stressful situations, such as a physical injury or other life setbacks, is challenging. Excluding these circumstances, some peoples' mindset do not allow inner peace even when everything is logically fine.

I have encountered people who get riled up with minor things, seemingly losing their inner peace quickly. At least, their outward behavior appears like that. They get angry or throw tantrums and generally exhibit all signs of losing their calm and inner peace in trivial situations.

There can be psychological explanations for this. One theme seems to be the overt exaggeration of their self-evaluated value in this World. The people who lose their inner peace quickly are probably overestimating their significance in this World, as a result of which, even the most minor inconvenience makes them think they are not getting something they are automatically entitled to.

An alternate psychological explanation can be that these people believe their value diminishes unless they fight for it; having that sense reduces inner peace.

Keeping with the theme of this book, let's borrow from some properties of the Universe and model inner peace according.

Thermodynamics of inner peace

Thermodynamics studies the relationships between heat, work, temperature, and energy. It describes how thermal energy is converted to and from other forms of energy and how thermal energy affects matter. The laws of thermodynamics describe how the energy in a system changes and whether the system can perform useful work on its surroundings.

Thermodynamics has three kinds of systems: Isolated, Closed, and Open:

An **Isolated system** is where neither matter nor energy can be exchanged. An example would be a thermos flask with hot water in it. Neither the water (matter) nor the energy (heat from the water) can escape it.

A **Closed system** is one where matter cannot be exchanged, but energy can be interchanged. An example of a Closed system would be water boiling in a pan with the lid tightly on. In this case, heat (energy) can be transferred out, but not the water (matter).

An **Open system** is one where both matter and energy can be exchanged. An example would be when the lid of the boiling pan is opened; water (matter) escapes as water vapor and heat (energy) escapes as well.

If the mind is a system, then we can model the mind as a Thermodynamic system, where information is equivalent to energy, and inner peace is equivalent to matter. To obtain a balanced inner peace in our mind, we want information and awareness to be exchangeable with our surroundings (energy), not our inner peace (matter).

Ideally, our mind should be a Closed system; it should be willing to exchange ideas, information, and awareness (energy) but not ready to exchange inner peace (matter) (**Figure 3.2**).

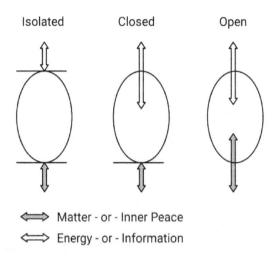

Figure 3.2. *Isolated, Closed and Open Thermodynamic system*

Modeling the mind as a Closed system leads to several interesting observations. The first and foremost is the one we just derived: inner peace cannot escape the system, which means, if your mind is like a Closed Thermodynamic system, then you are ready to absorb information and awareness around you, about your surroundings, about the people, about the situation you are in. With a Closed system, although information and awareness are exchanged, inner peace is shielded within your mind.

One thing to note is that inner peace is more of a longer-term average than an instantaneous state. You are expected to react to negative situations; obtaining a continuous and permanent state of inner peace is impossible. This is similar to a practical Thermodynamic system; in reality, they can leak matter and energy, such as a thermos flask content eventually cooling down due to a natural energy leak.

For example, negative situations can make you angry, scared, sad, or invoke subtle emotions. These are natural reactions to shock. The idea of inner peace, though, is not the fact that you respond naturally to a negative situation; instead, it is a measure of your *tolerance* to adversarial conditions; the more tolerance you have, the more inner peace you are capable of holding, and hence, your mind mimics the more 'true' Closed Thermodynamic system; not perfect, but close enough.

Making our mind react like a Closed Thermodynamic system is ideal and, through practice, can be achieved. Let's look at inner force vs external force. A solid ball will be less likely to succumb to external forces; for example, a soccer ball gets kicked around but has enough longevity to hold its shape for an entire match or more. Conversely, a balloon will quickly succumb to external forces and burst or get punctured. A stable form is attained when internal forces counter external forces. If the internal force is strong enough, more external force is required to deform the shape. A soccer ball is such an example. Similarly, if the inner force is weak, then a low amount of external force can dent the form; the balloon is such an example.

One parallel we can draw to keep our minds a Closed Thermodynamic system is to have a strong enough inner force so that external forces cannot damage and leak our minds' container.

If life gives external force, we should have enough internal force to not succumb to the pressures of life and the Universe. Following this principle, we can model our minds as a Closed system.

Entanglement and Inner Peace

People are a key factor of external forces trying to dent into our internal forces and break down our Closed, Thermodynamically modeled minds. Looking back at the concept of "entanglement" defined in the previous chapter, we are somehow entangled with other human beings; entanglement of any form, direct or indirect, can profoundly affect our inner peace. It can be a direct chain reaction or a long-winded indirect reaction.

For example, you can get affected by somebody misbehaving with you for no apparent reason. Children sometimes get bullied at school by their peers, directly affecting their inner peace. As social beings, we can get bullied by society. At work, we can get bullied by our bosses, colleagues, and others. Besides bullying, people can adversely affect you in any situation, even if you don't know them. Somebody can hurt you physically or damage your property. These are direct forms of entanglement and their effects.

As we saw in the last chapter, entanglement can be between unrelated people too. One example is daily commute woes due to heavy traffic, leading to stress, loss of health, and unhappiness. The commuters causing the traffic daily on the highway are people you don't know. Yet, you are *entangled* with them since they are also part of the cause of the traffic affecting you. Everybody in that traffic is entangled with each other and indirectly affects each other's Happiness.

One way or another, we are so entangled with people that it seems hard to detach. Their actions or inactions, directly or indirectly, will affect you. You cannot isolate yourself from this effect because we are all primarily social beings and mostly live near humans (with exceptions).

What is the best way to maintain a Closed Thermodynamic system of mind and hold on to our inner peace when being affected due to direct or indirect entanglement with humans is inevitable? Detachment lets you keep your mind behaving like a Closed Thermodynamic system and improve at obtaining inner peace. Let's elaborate on that a bit.

Detachment

Detachment is a crucial mental trick to induce inner peace and model the mind as a Closed Thermodynamic system. I say it's a "trick" because, in reality, due to direct or indirect "entanglement," you cannot practically disengage or detach from people and their effects on you. Sure, one may argue about the great Monks from Asian cultures and their teaching about detachment. But then, they can detach literally; they shun their families and friends. That is an extreme form of detachment. In reality, that is hard for most of us who are ordinary social beings and want to belong to the typical social framework of family, friends, colleagues, community, etc.

I have observed that when I detach from people and situations, and with it, the illusion of "control," facing any adversarial situation becomes more manageable, helping me attain a better state of inner peace.

In popular culture, in many movies and books, a classic theme is around fairness and unfairness: how the protagonist faces mistreatment and adversarial behavior from people with whom they had been friendly. Facing hostility from people and situations is a common theme, and entanglement forms a common motif. It has happened to me several times, and I am sure the reader has also faced hostile and unpleasant behavior from people you least expected from. The only way to handle these situations is to detach and let go.

Practical Methods to Detach and Let Go to attain Inner Peace

The method of detaching and letting go is not necessarily spiritual (albeit there are elements of it), nor is it some abstract meditation method. A simple change in mindset can obtain it by shifting the perspective.

Letting go is an actionable item. It can be an actual mental framework that enables you to have inner peace, create a protection shield around you, help you model your mind as a Closed system, and cause you less distress for situations you are not in control of. Borrowing from well-established social norms, here are some pragmatic methods for detaching and letting go (again, I am not a Happiness expert; this advice is just some practical ideas that I follow):

Avoid: Let go of the people who made you lose your inner peace repeatedly. If they did it once, they would do it again. Detach from them in all practical sense, and stay away from them because people's behavior hardly changes. Avoid them. Look out for warning signals in every interaction with them; those interactions can potentially harm you. Make a mental model of letting them go, avoiding them (as pleasantly as possible), and avoiding engaging in any interaction.

Erase memory: Let go of the memory which made you lose inner peace; it sounds difficult, but in reality, it is practical to detach from the past and learn from it, live for the present, and prepare for the future.

Neutralize negative energy: Let go of resentment associated with adverse events or people. That is the most challenging part. Resentment comes in unchecked and seems hard to control. Positive activities can mitigate resentment. Whenever resentment creeps in, it is a destructive energy. The idea is to quickly negate that with some positive actions that you like; go for a run, call somebody you like, watch a movie you enjoy, listen to your favorite music, or engage in any such activity that will let you negate the negative energy.

Change perspective: Shifting perspective is looking at the same situation differently. We looked at it briefly in the previous chapter. Looking at the problem or adversarial situation from a different perspective may seem less harmful. Somebody misbehaved with you: maybe they were having a bad day, or that particular event was stressful for them. Somebody bullies you: they are probably insecure or plain jealous of you. A forced change in perspective helps alleviate an adverse outcome and help in detaching from it.

Detachment and Happiness 3.0

Although detachment is a great technique to obtain inner peace, in practice, detachment is harder for Happiness 3.0. That is primarily due to the rich information and awareness associated with Happiness 3.0. Your social media feeds and all the personalized content will make it harder to detach yourself truly. If you lost the goodwill of a friend, who suddenly turned their back on you, you could have avoided them and moved on when there was no social media (Happiness 1.0). Now it may be challenging. They will still appear in your social feeds. They will appear to be friendly with everybody else but not with you. It will probably hurt you more. You see them enjoying time with others in your social media feeds, not with you, which will hurt. That's the way it works. You may still be wondering what happened. Detachment and letting go are the only way.

I have talked to several people who have completely detached from social media. From my theory, they are following Happiness 1.0 and moving away from Happiness 3.0. If it works well for them, that is an acceptable plan. That is a very effective way of detachment. They are detached from society's noise and the pain from seeing estranged relationships or feeling socially outcast.

However, detaching from social media seems harder for some people than others. I have often wondered about it and have concluded that many people suffer from **FOMO** (fear of missing out). Let's talk about FOMO a bit.

FOMO

With the help of our friend, Artificial Intelligence, social media is smartly personalizing content for you, showing content from friends and other social connections which will maximize your chances to engage with the content. Some people get addicted to this, and the key factor is FOMO. The fear of missing out on something that could have made them happy seems real and tangible.

There seem to be various examples of FOMO which is tangible today; here are a few:

Social Media FOMO: Seeing your friends posting about a fun event or party you were not invited to and feeling anxious and left out.

Travel FOMO: Seeing pictures of your friends or acquaintances on exotic vacations and missing out on unique experiences and adventures.

Product FOMO: Hearing about a limited-time sale or a new release of a popular product and feeling the urge to buy it immediately before it's unavailable.

Career FOMO: Seeing colleagues or peers achieving success or promotions in their careers and feeling pressured to keep up or fear being left behind.

Event FOMO: Hearing about a highly anticipated concert, festival, or party happening in your area and fearing missing out on a memorable experience or cultural moment.

Relationship FOMO: Observing friends or acquaintances in happy and fulfilling relationships and worrying about missing out on a similar connection.

Personal Achievement FOMO: Seeing others accomplish goals or milestones, such as running a marathon or starting a successful business, feeling pressured to achieve similar accomplishments, or fearing that you're falling behind.

Social FOMO: Being aware of gatherings or social events without your presence and fearing missing out on critical social interactions or bonding moments with friends or acquaintances.

FOMO is real and tangible and primarily affects Happiness 3.0. Notice the word **fear** in FOMO. It seems like a real fear! It is as real as, say, fear of height. It causes anxiety, stress and can directly affect your inner peace.

Reducing FOMO

What is a good way to reduce the anxiety and stress associated with FOMO? A difficult tactic is detaching yourself from all social circles' influence. That, however, is not a healthy option since social circles are necessary for your Happiness (we will talk more about that later in this chapter). On the other hand, when you mix with people in society, people are bound to talk about their little vacation and everything else, which can cause FOMO.

FOMO, though, is not a real issue for everybody. Some people are adaptive to others having fun without them, and they are OK with that. The key is, again, detachment; mental detachment, where it's OK to miss out. It is a complex state to achieve, but certainly possible.

This brings out an interesting perspective we can look at using the Happiness formula from the last chapter. Recall the Happiness formula from Chapter 2; the Happiness formula essentially says:

$$happiness = \frac{What\ you\ have}{What\ you\ desire}$$

Lowering one's desire to have all the 'fun' (which other people keep talking about) will increase Happiness. It is easier said than done, but it does boil down to having a simplistic and realistic viewpoint.

One interesting perspective for detachment is that if one needs to detach from people and circumstances that cause unhappiness, does one need to attach to something else? After all, we need to root out energy somewhere. In that light, attaching to the current state, and detaching from alternate states, is optimal. For example, your current state is that you are sitting at home watching TV with your family. The alternate state is that a large social circle is having a fun party, and you could have been at that party, just that you somehow missed it.

The idea is to attach to the current state (enjoy your time at home with your family) and detach from the alternate state (who cares what the others are doing?). Sure, if you see a picture of them having fun in your social media feed after some time, you would understandably feel a bit down. But then, if you wisely attach to your current state, you could turn the table around and, instead, realize that you had a good time watching TV with your family at home. Again, it's all easy to say, harder to do. But it works.

It all comes to the concept of "inner" in inner peace; you live in your little physical reality; it's your life, time, thoughts, and consciousness. You live in the "inner" you. Unless you admit others into that "inner" you, chances are you will master inner peace and detachment.

Precision and Recall

FOMO was less of an issue for Happiness 1.0. Happiness 1.0 stemmed from direct interactions with humans and was sandboxed out of information. You need information and awareness of what's happening around you to have FOMO! With no social media or other online content methods pumped through your phone, you may not even know what you are missing out on. That has drawbacks; recall of events that could have enriched your lives would be low. But the positive side is higher precision; you were happier with your state because you had nothing to compare.

I threw in the mathematical terms precision and recall casually in this current discussion; let us look at these two terms more closely because these are compelling metrics one needs to optimize.

To understand precision and recall in the context of Happiness, look at **Figure 3.3**. In this example, precision is the ratio of events that made you happy (H) out of all the events that you did. Recall is the number of events that made you happy out of all the events that *could have* made you happy.

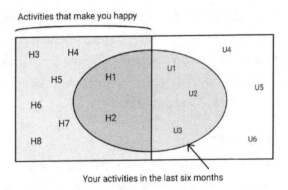

Figure 3.3. Precision Recall

Another example: consider a baby learning the seven colors. Suppose she is asked to name the colors. She says three words, all of which are colors. In this case, her precision is 100%, and her recall is three out of seven.

FOMO: maximize recall over precision

FOMO occurs due to our innate desire to *maximize recall over precision*. Let's look at an example to figure this out more intuitively. Suppose there are five events on a single day. You would try to maximize *precision* if you choose only a few events, or perhaps just one event on that day, which would make you happy, and stay in that event the entire day (which means you miss all the other events). As an alternate, you would try to maximize *recall* if you hopped to all the events where you felt you would have been happy.

If you optimize for recall most of the time, you are driven by FOMO.

Hopping to all invitations you have, trying to attend anything and everything going around, and trying to do everything that could have made you happy indicates an intense FOMO. Of course, there can be other interpretations because human beings are complex social beings.

Optimizing for precision or recall is an inherent trait that makes us behave in a certain way to maximize our Happiness.

Happiness 3.0 optimizes for Recall

Beyond just FOMO, it seems like Happiness 3.0 is more associated with *recall* than precision. The reason for this is the large, personalized information channel you have through social media and other Internet and digital media sources, all controlled and channeled by our friend, Artificial Intelligence. With all this information and social awareness presented serendipitously, you are aware of many other sources of Happiness, and you probably do many of those. This makes recall very high for Happiness 3.0, albeit, perhaps, at the cost of precision.

I have several examples to justify my theory that Happiness 3.0 is essentially optimizing for recall. My examples come from personal experiences.

For instance, media content providers like Netflix, YouTube, and others, keep recommending all kinds of content to me by personalizing it to my taste; content that would have been impossible to even know about if our friend, Artificial Intelligence, had not carefully personalized it for me and thrown my way through the content provider feeds. These personalized contents have increased my recall significantly; I can now consume far more content that makes me happy, compared to my childhood days of Happiness 1.0 when I just consumed what my friends told me, or which I obtained through other static sources of information.

In my school years, during the era of Happiness 1.0, I had no idea that so much delightful content, *which could have made me happy*, existed. In other words, Happiness 1.0 was limited to such an extent that I didn't even know what I was missing out on!

Recall was extremely low for Happiness 1.0. Back then, information was sandboxed. I did not know about the rich World of beautiful content from all around the World; beautiful music, movies, art, cultures, and stories.

But now, it's all there, carefully fed to me through Netflix, YouTube, TikTok, Facebook, and many other media networks, which directly contribute to my Happiness 3.0.

Through all this, I am automatically optimizing my recall; i.e., I am now consuming many more life experiences that can make me happy—experiences which, had I not known about them, would be a huge miss. I am happy every day that my friend, Artificial Intelligence, is here to cater to me personally, to know me personally, and give me great sources of joy which I had otherwise never known.

Happiness 3.0, thus, is all about optimizing recall with the combined help of Artificial Intelligence and smartphones.

Recall has gone up dramatically for all of us. Due to the constant and continuous personalized information around us through digital means channeled by Artificial Intelligence, we all have a much richer idea of where to travel, what to do, what to wear, what to watch, whom to follow, etc.

Purpose

Having talked about inner peace and detachment, a key question arises: if detachment is a way of protecting your inner peace, there must be some attachment to other aspects. After all, humans need a reason to wake up every day. Everybody needs to have a purpose in life. Not one purpose even, multiple purposes.

The equation becomes interesting now: you detach and attach simultaneously! Essentially, detach from outcomes that depend on others, and attach to outcomes where you are more in control. That is an ideal formula.

Returning to the issue of FOMO, a crucial differential to Happiness 3.0, there is a way to optimize purpose. By attaching to *you* and detaching from *them*, you are already a step ahead in optimizing inner peace and finding a purpose.

Purpose varies a lot between individuals. It varies so dramatically that it takes an entire analysis and thesis to pinpoint, cluster, and annotate the different types. Even within one person, the purpose may vary depending on the concentration. But it's safe to say that purpose plays a crucial role in Happiness.

Purpose and Happiness are interconnected concepts that can significantly influence well-being and fulfillment.

Let's look at what purpose means anyways.

Purpose refers to having a sense of meaning, direction, and significance in one's life. It involves identifying and pursuing goals, values, and activities that align with one's core beliefs and passions. A clear purpose provides a sense of direction, motivation, and a framework for decision-making. It gives individuals a sense of identity, allows them to contribute to something larger than themselves, and fosters a sense of fulfillment and satisfaction.

Having a sense of purpose can contribute significantly to one's Happiness. When individuals feel that their actions and choices align with their values and contribute to a greater purpose, they tend to experience a more profound sense of fulfillment, contentment, and Happiness. Purpose provides a sense of meaning and direction, which can help you navigate challenges, overcome obstacles, and find greater satisfaction in your daily lives.

There are anecdotal examples in everybody's life. From my childhood, I can take a throwback look at summer vacations. Like most children, I looked forward to summer vacations. When summer vacations eventually came, it was an ecstatic feeling. I could take on a life like the gardener for most of the summer: laze around all day, do simple stress-free activities and be relaxed, lazy, and happy.

In reality, though, a listlessness invariably crept in after the first few weeks when I had relaxed just enough.

That was when the need for a purpose arose.

Every day was purposeless during those long summers! I would get bored, and eventually, near the end of the summer vacations, when I was done with all the summer travels and randomly playing with friends, building cardboard robots, sketching, and playing music, I would yearn for a clear, discernable purpose. As a result, when school reopened, it made me happy because then, I had a purpose; to go to school, have a routine, go to a new class, make new friends, and learn new things.

Having a purpose seems essential to have a stable metric of Happiness. It is more of a tactic than something which directly affects your Happiness. Unlike inner peace, which is sometimes harder to control and manage, having a purpose is a relatively structured process.

Purpose plays a more prominent role in Happiness 3.0 than in its earlier versions. My argument for this is that there are more distractions from the Internet and digital content, social media, and all that; we looked at FOMO as an example. In that light, it is possible to get lost in a purposeless meandering, getting sucked into the distractions of the World of the Internet and personalized content.

Without a purpose, one can get sucked into endlessly consuming digital, personalized content without a real purpose, wasting hours daily with no result. This lack of purpose is seen in the current generation of younger adults, who are spending a tremendous amount of time chatting with their friends over the Internet in chatting Apps, watching YouTube or TikTok all day, and engaging in purposeless activities. Whether this is inherently harmful is debatable because, as we saw, chatting with friends gives you a social connection to reduce some of the FOMO, and watching online videos can certainly increase knowledge and awareness of world issues. At the same time, it does take away a more concrete purpose.

Does that inherently mean that our friend, Artificial Intelligence, is directly causing us to lose purpose and engage ourselves in consuming digital content purposelessly? It can be an argument of sorts.

Purpose is defined by the stage of life one is in. For young people, an essential purpose is to obtain a solid education, maintain physical activities to stay fit, and optimize the right amount of social interactions to stay social, yet not overdo it by wasting time chatting with friends all day. As we grow up, the purpose should be around making ourselves beneficial to society and our immediate family in several ways. For most adults, it means providing for the family by having jobs, businesses, etc. Parents have a vital purpose to make the best resources available to their children.

Purpose is also related to influence. Let's look at an interesting concept called the *circle of influence*.

Circle of influence

The **circle of influence (Figure 3.4)** defines the layers that define a person. Every individual is layered. Each layer provides a purpose.

Figure 3.4. *Circle of Influence*

The innermost core is **you**: your thoughts, emotions, likes and dislikes, dreams, wistfulness; essentially everything and anything that defines you. That is a very inner core, which only you can access. You influence your own self deeply. Only you can decide what you want, what makes you happy. Your fundamental purpose is to pursue your duties as an individual, and while doing so, try to be happy.

The immediate layer after that is your **immediate loved ones**, people who matter to you; it may be your family, very close friends, or anybody who can influence you the strongest. They provide you with another layer of purpose; to be there for them when required, provide them support and help when needed.

The third layer is your **friends and colleagues** who influence you. With friends, your purpose is to be with them when they need you. Work takes up a lot of our time, and, understandably, your colleagues with whom you work will significantly influence your life. Your immediate boss will affect it and is easily the most important person in your career. As the saying goes, when people leave companies, they don't leave the company but their boss. Conversely, having a great boss means you will likely be happy in your career.

The same goes for colleagues: having great colleagues makes up for work stress; they will share it with you, and your career will be happy. This entire layer provides a purpose of work for you: work that sustains you, provides for you and your family, and also, is a crucial source of satisfaction if it goes well.

The next layer is your local **community**; your community may be people you mix with socially at large, an actual community where you live, or any generally defined set of people with whom you associate in a larger setting. It may be people who speak your language in your region, or of the same belief system, or however you define it. You have a larger purpose of contributing to your community directly or indirectly through community contributions, donations, and volunteering work.

The next layer is your **"clan"** across the World. How do you even know about people around the World who align with your thoughts, the common language you speak, or some other common theme? With global connectivity, social media feeds, and other personalized information sources, you are connected with people similar to you in some aspects across the World. You may not even know them personally, but you share the same sense of identity.

I can take my example; through Facebook groups, I am connected to several people across the World who share the same interests as me or speak the same language as I do and share the same culture. I have never seen them; yet, they influence me a lot and belong to my circle of influence. These people are my "clan" across the World.

My "clan" gives me a purpose to hold on to my lineage, language, culture, etc.

The final layer is your **global belongingness**. You are human, and all humans have some common threads which bind them together. A significant catastrophic event in any part of the World will likely make you feel concerned or sad, to various extents, irrespective of which language you speak, which "clan" you associate with, or any such clusters.

I was a college student when 9/11 happened in the USA in 2001. I had never come to the USA then and was not directly connected with anybody in the USA. Yet, it shocked me, made me sad, and all my peers were equally shocked and dismayed. Possibly a majority of people across the World were shocked as the Twin Towers collapsed. There is something global about it; the typical feeling of anxiety and concern that surpasses all other clustering of humans by clans or communities of friends or loved ones.

We have a duty towards the planet where we live. As global citizens, we have a responsibility and purpose to be actively aware of anything that can add to global warming or pollution and curb those—driving electric cars and taking public transportation when possible. Ride a bicycle. Walk. Pick up trash left over. Not pollute water bodies, the forests, the lands, and trees that give us shelter and a place called home.

The different versions of Happiness connect differently with these circles of influence. Happiness 1.0 is directly tied with the inner circle of you, close friends, and then friends and colleagues. It becomes more versioned in the outer layers, especially if you look at your "clan" around the Globe and your belongingness in a global world. Happiness 3.0 is more relevant to these outer layers.

Having talked about two relatively abstract concepts: inner peace and purpose, let's look at a more tangible impact on Happiness: **wealth**. In the Happiness tree model in **Figure 3.1**, I have bucketed both material and nonmaterial wealth in the same bucket. There are compelling reasons for that. Let's look at material wealth, to begin with.

Material Wealth and Happiness

A classical proverb that I, and possibly most of us, have heard all our lives is: 'Money cannot buy you Happiness.' There can be countless arguments over it. The meaning of the proverb needs to be clarified, to begin with. Is Happiness something that can be bought? Does having more wealth equate to more Happiness? Does having less wealth equate to having less Happiness? The answers to these are very circumstantial and relative, with several aspects of introspection.

Instead, the argument that 'Money cannot buy you Happiness' can be reframed as a question: 'Is wealth required for happiness?'

Not having sufficient wealth to sustain can lead to profound unhappiness; that's a given, and we can observe that in popular culture and anecdotally. At the same time, having wealth beyond comfortable requirements does not necessarily mean an increase in Happiness.

The above popular proverb probably considers aspects beyond money that lead to Happiness, such as social well-being, social connection, having a family to turn to, and other factors. But the question remains: does money bring Happiness?

Let's consider another question: are people from wealthy nations generally happier than people from less wealthy nations? Or is there no correlation? That is hard to say at an individual level, albeit studies have shown some correlation. The World Happiness Index measures subjective well-being based on various factors such as economic prosperity, social support, personal freedom, and levels of corruption.

While wealth is one of the factors considered when calculating the World Happiness Index, research has shown a correlation between wealth and Happiness is not as high as expected. Beyond a certain income level, additional income does not necessarily lead to a corresponding increase in Happiness.

Some countries that consistently rank high on the World Happiness Index, such as Finland, Denmark, and Switzerland, are not necessarily the wealthiest in the World. These countries have robust social support systems, high levels of trust and freedom, and a sense of community that contributes to their citizens' well-being.

Happiness from wealth beyond a certain basic standard, such as providing enough to sustain housing, education, food, a safety net to get by with the amenities required for life, and occasional entertainment, turns out to be relative.

However, therein lies the dilemma; considerable wealth is necessary to have a comfortable house and buy things you want. If you are a parent, you need to be comfortably wealthy to send your kids to the schools you want to. For your comfort and occasional entertainment, you need sufficient wealth to go to restaurants when you want to, buy home improvements as and when you want to, go for vacations, and watch concerts.

Thus, another way of looking at it is to observe that unhappiness can be primarily curbed with sufficient wealth.

In a Utopian world, there would be sufficient wealth for everybody so that at least unhappiness due to lack of wealth would disappear (albeit there are arguments against it, as we discussed in the previous chapter). Wealth distribution around the Globe, though, is far from utopic.

According to the World Inequality Report, an average adult individual earns USD 23,380 per year in 2021, and the average adult owns USD 102,600. Or in other words, an average person's annual income is one-fifth of what they owe. These averages, however, mask wide disparities both between and within countries. The wealthiest 10% of the global population currently takes 52% of global income. In contrast, the poorest half earns 8.5% of it.

On average, an individual from the top 10% of the worldwide income distribution earns USD 122,100 per year. In contrast, an individual from the poorest half of the global income distribution makes USD 3,920.

Global wealth inequalities are even more pronounced than income inequalities. The poorest half of the worldwide population barely owns any wealth, possessing just 2% of the total. In contrast, the wealthiest 10% of the global population owns 76% of all wealth.

Are these 10% global population with so much wealth the happiest of the lot, above the rest of the 90% population? World Happiness does not indicate this disparity of wealth. There must be something beyond wealth, then.

Taking cues from my childhood, just having enough food, a place to sleep, and, most importantly, lots of friends from school and the neighborhood made me happy, and probably most children around me. There was no question of having wealth; meager pocket money was the norm. Yet, as far as I remember, my childhood was tremendously happy.

Let's look at our friends, the gardener, and the CEO. The CEO is presumably wealthy, so there should only be an issue if he is one of those early-stage startup CEOs who does not get paid but has significant ownership of a company that he hopes will fetch a dividend sometime. We will not get into that. Now, consider the gardener. It's all well to say; he is so relaxed and peaceful. There lies a lot of invisible background here:

1. The gardener has a job!
2. He brings lunch, which means he can afford food.
3. He can afford to be relaxed without ambition, which means he does not need money for sustenance.
4. He probably has a home to visit or a place to stay.
5. He can work, commute, sleep, and eat, so he probably has no significant physical disabilities.

These are already tremendous privileges to have! Consider home prices in Silicon Valley, California, to put things into perspective. Admittedly, it is one of the most expensive places in the World to stay. But putting a spin on it, the 1990s saw a significant increase in home prices, driven by the dot-com boom. Silicon Valley home prices have continued to rise, fueled by a growing technology industry and a shortage of available housing. As of summer 2023, the median home price in Silicon Valley is around $1.4 million, making it one of the most expensive housing markets in the country.

To have a reasonably good life in Silicon Valley, families must either work hard to make decent money to survive or inherit wealth. The latter is relatively rare, so families in Silicon Valley need to work hard to sustain themselves. One can think of the CEO and equate things there. But how about the gardener? Could an average Silicon Valley person laze around, do nothing, earn a little bit, sleep all day, and get to live by? It seems unlikely.

Yet, the gardener seemed happy and relaxed. That was because the hardships of acquiring wealth were taken care of for him. It was almost the case that I mentioned just before; acquiring wealth. The fact that the gardener could do almost nothing yet get to live means that he does not have to take the stress of acquiring wealth, shelter, clothing, food, etc. It came easily from some source unknown to the CEO, whatever it might be, as a result of which he could get by doing nothing.

One can argue that the gardener's desires were less; hence, Happiness was higher, as per the Happiness formula. However, there is a constant need for all humans; food, shelter, and clothing. However much one may claim to shun the material World, in reality, without these three basic requirements, humans cannot survive.

Looks like these basics for sustenance were taken care of comfortably for the gardener, and he was happy with the basics.

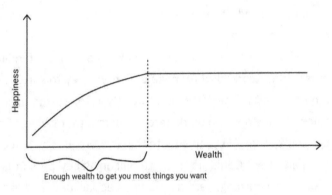

Figure 3.5. Wealth Happiness Relationship

Figure 3.5 shows the relationship between Happiness and wealth. Based on our discussions, wealth contributes to Happiness, but to a certain degree, after which it does not impact significantly.

Happiness formula and wealth

Does the Happiness formula adhere to the model of Happiness in **Figure 3.1**? It implies that it does. Let's look at wealth and the Happiness formula. Continuing our example from the previous chapter, for a child born in an underprivileged household, getting a proper meal daily or accessing decent healthcare, accommodation, and education is a happy thought. These aspects can fit in some parts of the Happiness tree model in **Figure 3.1**. In this case, the Happiness formula would read like so:

$$happiness(\text{underprivileged child}) =$$
$$\frac{Has\ basic\ food, education, shelter}{Desire\ to\ get\ food, education, shelter}$$

It is simple to interpret this formula. If the child has the basics of food, shelter, and education and desires it, they are happy. Simple enough. Maximizing the underprivileged child's Happiness seems easy by simply providing basic food, education and a shelter. If this child gets more than what they expected, their Happiness increases. If they desire beyond the basics, their Happiness decreases.

The same cannot be said of a child born to a reasonably wealthy family; having basic food and access to education and shelter is not a novelty for them. The Happiness formula has an extra factor, called 'other':

$$happiness(\text{privileged child}) =$$
$$\frac{Has\ basic\ food, education, shelter + other}{Desire\ to\ get\ basic\ food, education, shelter + other}$$

The additional 'other' parameter beyond basic food, education, and shelter makes it exponentially more complicated.

If this child gets the basics of food, shelter, and education, and nothing much beyond that, they will understandably be unhappy; in fact, much more unhappy than the underprivileged child whose desire is just the basics of food, shelter, and education.

But at the same time, it is understandable that wealth, which is available to the more privileged child, will enable them to get the 'other' somewhat; their Happiness will go up.

At some point, comparing absolute Happiness, much less wealth is required to make the underprivileged child 'happy' than the more privileged one. Of course, this does not speak of anything about the privileged child's attitude. The child is conditioned to their circumstance of wealth or lack thereof. Having enough wealth to discern these fundamental rights of the child is certainly not the cause of unhappiness. But for the child from an underprivileged family, the 'other' is an extra, making them much happier than the privileged child getting that extra 'other.' Even a little bit of extra wealth can make an underprivileged child much happier than a regular privileged one; or, in terms of Happiness measurement discussed in the previous chapter:

$$happiness_{Wealth}(underprivileged\ child) >$$
$$happiness_{Wealth}(privileged\ child)$$

In this case, wealth makes the underprivileged child happier. But then, if the underprivileged child gets sustained wealth, do they remain underprivileged? I will skip that discussion for the reader to ponder upon.

Artificial Intelligence and Wealth

From our discussions, wealth does increase Happiness, at least to some extent. Artificial Intelligence can benefit wealth generation.

A.I. can drive innovation by enabling enterprises to discover new insights, uncover hidden patterns, and identify untapped market opportunities. By leveraging A.I. in research and development, companies can accelerate product development, create novel solutions, and gain a competitive edge, leading to increased profitability and wealth generation. By leveraging AI-powered analytics, companies can identify market trends and customer preferences and optimize their strategies to capitalize on opportunities, enhance customer satisfaction, and drive revenue growth.

A.I. technologies like chatbots, virtual assistants, and personalized recommendations can enhance customer experiences. By providing personalized and tailored services, AI-powered systems can improve customer satisfaction, increase customer retention rates, and drive sales.

A.I. algorithms can analyze complex financial data, identify patterns, and make predictions. This capability can be particularly valuable in stock trading, risk assessment, fraud detection, and investment strategies, helping businesses and investors make informed financial decisions and potentially increase their wealth.

Health and Happiness

It does not take a lot of thinking to realize that lack of good health can certainly ebb away Happiness significantly. Who wants to be unhealthy and suffer? One can take care of their physical well-being by trying to keep fit according to age. Health may deteriorate due to external factors, such as chronic illness. That certainly ebbs away from Happiness. It is safe to say that health contributes to one's Happiness.

Wealth and health have some relationship. We can see that in the extremes, such as underprivileged children being malnutrition, with much less life expectancy, than relatively privileged children.

The Global or national health Index tool measures the overall health status of countries around the World. The index considers factors such as life expectancy, infant mortality rate, prevalence of communicable and non-communicable diseases, access to healthcare, and environmental factors. Several organizations publish global health indices, including the World Health Organization (WHO), the United Nations Development Programme (UNDP), and the Institute for Health Metrics and Evaluation (IHME).

One of the most widely used global health indices is the Global Health Security Index. It was developed by the Nuclear Threat Initiative (NTI) and the Johns Hopkins Center for Health Security. This index measures a country's ability to prevent, detect, and respond to health emergencies like pandemics or bioterrorism. Another essential global health index is the Human Development Index (HDI) , which the UNDP developed. This index considers health status, education, and income levels to provide a more comprehensive measure of a country's development.

The relationship between the wealth of a nation and its national health index is complex and multifaceted. Generally, there is a positive correlation between a country's wealth and health index, meaning that countries with higher economic development tend to have better health outcomes.

One reason for this correlation is that wealthier nations are often able to invest more resources into healthcare infrastructure, research and development, and disease prevention and treatment. They may also have better access to clean water and sanitation, which can reduce the prevalence of infectious diseases.

However, this relationship is complex; many factors can influence a country's health index beyond its economic wealth.

For example, social and environmental factors such as education, income inequality, air pollution, and healthcare access can significantly impact health outcomes. Additionally, many examples of countries with lower levels of economic development have achieved impressive gains in health outcomes through innovative healthcare delivery and disease prevention approaches.

Artificial Intelligence and Health

Artificial Intelligence has been used in healthcare for several decades. Still, its application in recent years has been significant due to advancements in computational power and the availability of large amounts of healthcare data.

One of the earliest examples of A.I. in healthcare was the development of the MYCIN system in the early 1970s. MYCIN was an expert system that used rule-based reasoning to diagnose bacterial infections and suggest treatments.

In the 1980s, the use of A.I. in healthcare expanded to include image analysis, with the development of systems that could interpret medical images such as X-rays and C.T. scans. The development of these systems enabled radiologists to detect and diagnose abnormalities more accurately and efficiently.

In the 1990s, A.I. was used to develop decision support systems that could assist clinicians in making treatment decisions. These systems analyzed patient data to suggest treatment options based on the patient's symptoms and medical history. In the 2000s, A.I. began to be used in electronic health records (EHRs) to help with clinical decision-making. AI-powered EHRs could identify potential drug interactions and alert clinicians to adverse events.

More recently, A.I. has been used in healthcare to develop predictive disease diagnosis and treatment models.

Machine learning algorithms can analyze large amounts of patient data to identify patterns and predict disease outcomes, and can revolutionize healthcare by enabling earlier disease detection and more personalized treatment options.

Taking our measurement from the previous chapter, suppose John's health has remained the same from the pre-AI era and now. Given the remarkable advances and uses of A.I. to advance the state of healthcare, one can generalize that

$$happiness^{3.0}_{Health}(John) > happiness^{1.0}_{Health}(John)$$

That is, John's Happiness, when it comes to health, is possibly higher when it comes to Happiness 3.0 because now A.I. is directly or indirectly helping John to remain healthy through early diagnostics and other medical advances.

Non Material Wealth and Happiness

Non material wealth refers to aspects of life not necessarily tied to material possessions or financial wealth, such as personal relationships, social connections, and a sense of purpose and fulfillment. Non material wealth is the wealth of resources you have that material possessions cannot buy: friends, family, and community belongingness.

Growing up with close connections with friends from school, a hoard of cousins, and a community rich in culture and inclusiveness, I find the relationships built through these are great non material wealth. These relationships have always given me direct Happiness.

Our brains are designed to seek comfort from familiarity given by this non material wealth and automatically respond favorably to positive social interactions. A birthday celebration. Marriage of a cousin. A weekend get-together with some friends. A community event of culture and participation. Social interactions contribute directly to Happiness.

Social connections are a tremendous nonmaterial wealth. A decades long Harvard study on Happiness has proved that embracing community helps us live longer, and be happier. The study revealed that close relationships keep people happy more than money or fame. Those ties protect people from life's discontents, help to delay mental and physical decline, and are better predictors of long and happy lives than social class, I.Q., or even genes. That finding proved true across the board among the Harvard study and inner-city participants.

In a nutshell, social connections and being a "social fit" are essential to Happiness. As a child, I could not imagine a day without my friends from school, and kids from the local neighborhood. Growing up, the definition of a friend has changed somewhat, with the community and social circle expanding beyond work or neighborhood. But without a doubt, friends are a special part of every person, without whom life is a trifle dull.

Happiness 3.0 and Social Connectivity

Happiness 3.0 benefits from social connections more than its previous versions. Back when there was no digital technology, friendship could sustain with physical presence. Now, it is much easier to create and maintain social connections without physical proximity.

As a child, I used to ride on my bicycle for miles to meet up with friends living on the town's other side. There was no phone or WhatsApp to chat with them or video chat to ping them and come online. While that was a shortcoming, there was an organic touch to it. Friends were genuinely missed.

They still are today, but it's easier to phone, text, or get in touch with them in the myriad ways digital tech provides. It goes beyond that. A long-lost friend suddenly appears as a "suggested friend" on Facebook, changing the equation dramatically. Artificial Intelligence somehow figures out the connections between my existing friends and my other data points and figures out the link. Often, it is accurate.

I have connected with countless friends from my school days, college days, and other places on Facebook. It gives great joy to reunite after ages. Their pictures on their social media feeds give me a peek into their current lives and how they have, or have not, changed.

Happiness 3.0 is undoubtedly more prominently impacted by social connections. Our friend Artificial Intelligence is working hard to crisscross everybody into a common mess of humanity, connecting people with things in common.

I have a lot of friends now across the World, many of whom I have never seen in person. It makes me happy to see their growth, their activities. It makes me happy to exchange ideas and well wishes with them occasionally.

I also get to see many different cultures across the World. When my friends from Hong Kong share something on Facebook, such as a wedding picture, it amazes me. When my friends from England shares pictures of their kids, of their family hikes, it makes me happy.

It makes me even happier when I talk to them through messages and chats. I get a sense of connection to many people whom I can call friends. Over time, the friendships have blossomed to the extent that when I travel to their part of the World, they ask me to come and visit them. All this is part of Happiness 3.0.

Artificial Intelligence and Social Connectivity

We have discussed the general implications of Artificial Intelligence based personalization which makes social connections easier. A.I. algorithms play a significant role in social media platforms by analyzing user data and preferences to personalize content recommendations. We have talked about this aspect at length.

The power of A.I. to induce social connections goes beyond recommendations and personalization. For example, AI-powered communication tools like voice assistants and chatbots facilitate individual interactions and connectivity. They can help people stay connected with friends and family, provide instant responses to queries, and bridge the gap between individuals who may be physically distant. These A.I. technologies can enhance social connections by enabling more accessible and efficient communication.

A.I.-based matchmaking algorithms are used in online dating platforms to help individuals find compatible partners. By analyzing user preferences and behavior, A.I. can suggest potential matches, increasing the likelihood of forming meaningful social connections.

A.I.-powered social robots like Pepper or Buddy interact with humans and provide companionship. These robots can engage in conversations, recognize emotions, and offer assistance.

Freedom

Freedom is a fundamental human right that protects us from the domination of oppressive regimes or entities. Without freedom, our ability to decide for ourselves, pursue paths of our choosing, and express ourselves without fear of retribution is severely limited.

Freedom and human rights are closely linked. Human rights have continued to evolve. The first generation of human rights were civil and political rights. The second generation of human rights include economic, social, and cultural rights. The third generation of human rights is called solidarity rights. The United Nations has adopted more than 20 principal treaties, including conventions, to prevent and prohibit specific abuses like torture and genocide and to protect particularly vulnerable populations, such as refugees. The U.N. General Assembly adopted the Universal Declaration of Human Rights on 10 December 1948 due to the experience of the Second World War.

Freedom has a surprisingly strong effect on one's Happiness. At least, for me, and, to an extent, for most of the people I have known and interacted with, a constant source of unhappiness is a lack of freedom. Looking at it more broadly globally, freedom in the 21st century seems obvious. However, there are political geo regions within this planet that are strife in restricting freedom for women and minorities.

At an individual level, even if the lack of freedom is not at an entire level of the community, personal freedom can be hampered due to various factors. Some people get stuck in a career where they can't move, grow, or do what they want, leading to unhappiness. Some people are stuck in relationships where they lose their freedom. Freedom is an essential aspect of Happiness.

Does Happiness 3.0 come with more freedom? It is a complex and very personal question, with no direct answer without knowing the exact background and situation of the individual.

Are we really ever free?

Am I really free? I am sure my reader has pondered on this question at some point. Am I really, *really* free to do *exactly* what I want, be *exactly* what I want to be? Can I get up daily and tell myself I can do what pleases me? For most of us, there are restrictions.

When the significant aspects of human rights and freedom have been solved, the more minor elements of freedom are often lacking, shackling us to a life that could be more optimal. Do we have to work for a living? Why can't I be on an eternal vacation, traveling the World, being with my family at every moment, playing music when and where I want to, and doing exactly what I want, be where I want to be?

Conversely, are most of us happy with our jobs? Do we have the freedom to choose the optimum career choice in terms of company, location or in terms of team, or boss? For some, maybe, but I suspect it is not optimal for most people.

It looks like freedom takes on a whole new dimension which dramatically affects our Happiness. As we grow up, freedom is slowly taken away from us as responsibilities, expectations, and requirements from family and society start shackling us to a life that follows a narrower line; this is akin somewhat to the thin line of Happiness 1.0, which is sandboxed and limited.

One aspect of Happiness 3.0 is the serendipitous discovery of people across the World who have obtained the freedom to pursue exactly what they want. It happens all the time with me when I go on social media. Once in a while, I come across someone who pursues exactly what their passion is. That makes me wonder whether I would ever reach that state of doing exactly what I wanted, especially in my career.

Technology has undoubtedly opened up avenues for freedom of choice of career. With personalized feeds by A.I. showing us a constant stream of career options in professional social media like LinkedIn, perhaps the choice, and more importantly, awareness about career choices, has expanded significantly. There is more freedom to discover and choose a career of choice.

Freedom manifests differently in different regions of the World.

In some countries and territories, women have substantially less freedom regarding education choices and economic opportunities than men. Due to the inherent political divide, financial freedom is significantly less for a specific section of people in some other regions.

Colorism, racism, and sexism are rampant in some parts of this planet, which shackle people and deprive them of their freedom to obtain seemingly innocuous and essential opportunities to pursue a life of their choice.

Happiness 3.0, subjected to a torrent of awareness and digital information, is better posed to enjoy a boost from freedom. Awareness and information go a long way in opening up avenues of freedom for the less privileged.

Artificial Intelligence and Freedom

Beyond the subtle effects of A.I. on us discovering more means of freedom through awareness, A.I. can directly help people with limited physical freedom due to disability. Artificial Intelligence can improve accessibility for people with disabilities by providing assistive technologies. Natural language processing, computer vision, and other A.I. techniques enable individuals with visual or hearing impairments to interact with digital content, expanding their freedom to access and engage with information.

Protecting Happiness

Earth seems ripe with the possibility of life springing anywhere and everywhere. As discussed in Chapter 1, Happiness and joy are abundant in this Universe. At the same time, paradoxically, Happiness is limited, not infinite.

Despite Happiness and joy being abundant, it is critical to protect that Happiness so that predators do not take it away. Protecting Happiness must be covered by something other than the five key pillars in the Happiness tree model.

The history of humanity is rife with events known to cause disastrous robbing of Happiness. Occasional wars, crimes, brutality, oppression, division, prejudices and discrimination is rampant in a planet where Happiness is, paradoxically, abundant and enough for everybody.

Protecting Happiness is like protecting our assets and property. Some crimes are direct, and can be dealt with a proper structure. At home, we install security devices such as cameras and other services. Valuables are stowed away in bank lockers. Our bank account online transactions and logins are secured through passwords, multi-factor authorization, and other Internet security protocols. Credit card companies have fraud detection technology and processes to detect when somebody steals our credit card information and uses that to use our money to buy their stuff.

All these are tangible and measurable crimes that directly affect our assets. Happiness is such an asset itself, an essential asset that cannot be materially seen or felt. Yet, it has all the properties of being a physical entity.

Happiness, too, needs security protocols to be protected, similar to how tangible assets like property and wealth are protected. Happiness needs to be stowed away in safe places where social bullies and human sociopaths cannot rob it.

Suppose there was a hypothetical company that took care of Happiness, similar to how credit cards are taken care of by banks. What would that company employ as safety measures?

It would use systems to ensure our friends are not stolen from us, and our reputation is not falsely targeted.

It would look out for social bullies who target us, try to shun us from society, falsely tarnish our image, and essentially rob us of Happiness by targeting those non-tangible but essential-for-life assets to make us unhappy.

Unfortunately, these kinds of social crimes which rob us of our Happiness are challenging to gauge. No companies, banks, or other institutions can take care of them for us, unlike material wealth. There is no earthly body to keep a tab on that; there are no judges, courts, or laws to stop our Happiness from getting robbed this way.

Happiness needs to be protected against social bullies who can rob our Happiness. Bullying is prevalent everywhere in society. Social alienation and friend stealing are common themes in communities where the bullies decide who should be included in society and who should not. It seems it is human nature to dominate.

Bullying starts at school, even with young children who are not exposed to social norms that much. About 20% of students ages 12-18 in the USA experienced bullying nationwide. Students aged 12–18 who reported being bullied said they thought those who bullied them could influence other students' perception of them (56%), had more social influence (50%), were physically stronger or larger (40%), or had more money (31%).

How does one protect one's Happiness? It seems like an eternally tricky question. A corresponding protection tactic can be utilized for each of the pillars in the Happiness model.

For some of the pillars, the ways of protection are rather obvious.

For material wealth, there are well-established safeguards.

For physical health, there are well-established methods; regular checkups, exercising, quitting toxic intake through food or chemicals, getting proper rest and sleep, proper nutrients through diets, and such.

The protection mechanism is more complex for the other pillars of inner peace, purpose, freedom, and nonmaterial wealth, such as social connections. As we discussed, no institutes, companies, or established laws or methods exist to protect these. Yet, they have a significant, tangible effect on one's Happiness and certainly need protection mechanisms.

A synopsis

We have seen a tree model of Happiness, with five pillars: inner peace, purpose, health, wealth, and freedom contributing majorly to Happiness. Optimizing each of these key five pillars would lead to optimizing Happiness. Artificial Intelligence can play an important role in optimizing each of these pillars, thus effectively optimizing Happiness 3.0.

How will Artificial Intelligence evolve in the near future? Will it continue being an integral part of our daily lives through personalization and smartphones, as it is today, and help us attain Happiness 3.0?

Or could it evolve beyond something we can discern at this moment? Do we need some global standardization to reign in the power of A.I. lest it become too sublime for us to control and manage?

Let's conclude our discussions in this book with these topics in the final next chapter.

CHAPTER 4

---^---

A.I. Singularity and Happiness

Our friend, Artificial Intelligence, is here for good. There is no denying it. It is present in all aspects of digital technology that we deal with daily regularly, primarily through smartphones, smart speakers, and smart displays.

As of summer 2023, its effect on common culture is subtle, aiding us gently with personalized recommendations through digital content. Artificial Intelligence is also present in other technological manifestations, such as self-driving cars, robot vacuums, and such, to make our lives easier. These have made our lives simpler and have affected Happiness 3.0 directly or indirectly, sometimes known to us, sometimes unknowingly.

The advent of omnipresent and personalized digital content, personalized and customized by Artificial Intelligence, has brought a dramatically broadened perspective to all of us. It has mixed world cultures and world views, mashing things together into one idea of humanity. Language, cultural and geographical boundaries are dissolving as ideas and content from one culture seeps into the other through personalized recommendations and feeds.

With the nascent invention of sophisticated Artificial Intelligence language systems, such as Google Bard and Chat GPT, humanity's combined wisdom and knowledge is now ready to be presented in concise explanations at our fingertips. The fine boundary between what we know and should be knowing has started dissolving.

Biases and prejudices around culture, race, color and gender are slowly dissolving as knowledge and awareness about anything and everything is permeated through fine sieves of channelized information, creating new awareness and a sense of global oneness.

Behind all this, Artificial Intelligence subtly plays a significant role in shaping and channeling content to us through digital media.

While the manifestation of Artificial Intelligence is still at its nascent stages in real life, the outlook and representation of A.I. is somewhat different in popular culture. The day is close when Artificial Intelligence's manifestations for human beings will be beyond the personalized feeds in smartphones, self-driving cars, smart vacuum cleaners, etc.

The progress of A.I. development implies that the manifestations of Artificial Intelligence will be more profound sometime in the near future.

When that is so, will Artificial Intelligence take the form of another species that cohabit on this planet with us? If that is so, what will they manifest like? How will Artificial Intelligence affect our Happiness directly?

To discuss these, let's first look at the evolution of Artificial Intelligence.

Evolution of Artificial Intelligence

The idea of "a machine that thinks" dates back to ancient Greece, albeit technology had not advanced to materialize anything remotely intelligent. Things took a turn starting in the mid-twentieth century, when mass-scale computing, with the capability to process large amounts of data in fractions of seconds, became a reality.

In 1950, Alan Turing published "Computing Machinery and Intelligence", in which he proposes to answer the question, "Can machines think?" He introduced the Turing Test to determine if a computer can demonstrate the same intelligence, or the results of the same intelligence, as a human.

In 1956, John McCarthy, the future inventor of the Lisp programming language, coined the term 'Artificial Intelligence' at the first-ever A.I. conference at Dartmouth College. Later that year, Allen Newell, J.C. Shaw, and Herbert Simon created the Logic Theorist, the first-ever running artificial intelligence software program.

In 1958, Frank Rosenblatt built the Mark 1 Perceptron, the first computer based on a neural network that 'learned' through trial and error. This computer was the pioneering effort to create a seed for modern deep learning-based A.I., which trains on data similarly.

In 1969, Marvin Minsky and Seymour Papert published a book titled *Perceptrons*, which became both the landmark work on neural networks and, at least for a while, an argument against future neural network research projects.

There was a brief lull in this period for A.I. It seems the masters of these technologies were busy advancing the capabilities, speed, memory, and usage of the computers, which would be the backbone of Artificial Intelligence. By the early 1980s, floppy drives and hard drives had been invented. The microprocessor, the heart of the computer, had advanced to excellent clock speeds. The IBM PC and BBC Micro were developed to take computers to the mainstream.

As computers slowly became mainstream in the 1980s, Neural networks, a critical under-the-hood learning technology used for A.I, emerged, and over time, became widely used in A.I. applications.

While I was reveling in my newfound source of Happiness in the late 1990s from surfing the Internet with the blue links given by Yahoo and Google, voraciously devouring the information from the World Wide Web and plunging myself into Happiness 2.0, serious strides in advancing Artificial Intelligence was happening in research institutes and tech companies all over the world to bring Artificial Intelligence to the mainstream.

As the common person worldwide became aware of the World Wide Web in the late 1990s, IBM demonstrated its expert system Artificial Intelligence computer called Deep Blue in 1996 which could play chess like a professional chess player.

Artificial Intelligence became a global and public phenomenon when, in 1996, IBM announced a live broadcast of its Deep Blue computer playing chess against the then-reigning human world chess champion, Garry Kasparov.

For the first time, Artificial Intelligence vs. Human Intelligence went to battle for the coveted title of superiority. People all over the world got interested in this competition.

Kasparov won the first match played in Philadelphia in 1996 by 4–2. Humans worldwide heaved a sigh of relief, albeit with less confidence than they would have hoped. After all, the A.I. machine won two out of the six matches!

Deep Blue won a rematch in New York City in 1997 by 3½–2½. The second match was the first defeat of a reigning world chess champion by a computer under tournament conditions. It was the subject of a documentary film, "Game Over: Kasparov and the Machine." With this match, Artificial Intelligence announced itself globally as a significant force that would evolve alongside humans from then on and, in time, would begin to influence their lives directly.

Soon, as expected, Artificial Intelligence started to be used for generally available digital technologies using the

Internet. Yahoo and Google began as search engines in the late 1990s. While they did not initially use Artificial Intelligence to power their search algorithms, they eventually incorporated A.I. techniques to improve their search results.

Google's initial search algorithm, PageRank, was based on the analysis of hyperlinks between web pages rather than Artificial Intelligence. Google has since incorporated machine learning and natural language processing techniques, core components of A.I. systems, to improve its search results, such as with its RankBrain algorithm.

As of 2023 today, almost all digital content providers use A.I. to power their algorithms to customize the content used for personalized recommendations, ad targeting, and natural language processing for voice assistants.

Look at your social media feeds, new channels, YouTube videos, feeds everywhere, and all the set of modern information and media apps, and you will notice that a majority of the content there is something you did not seek; it came you, carefully crafted by Artificial Intelligence based algorithms, to maximize your attention span and keep you hooked on to the app.

Artificial Intelligence started affecting humans when the Internet's reach for common people went beyond Internet searches and emails. With the advent of social networks, personalized feeds through news, and targeted recommendations in video sites and search results, the Internet evolved from just being a way to connect to websites to being a fundamental technology to target a large amount of personalized information to users.

Robots and Artificial Intelligence

The romanticizing of Artificial Intelligence in popular culture, through books and movies, is not new. Popular culture ties Artificial Intelligence with a physical form, especially to a human-like resemblance. The closest to humans are humanoid robots. As of now, in the summer of 2023, humanoid robots have evolved to a point where their physical behavior mimics real humans remarkably well.

Several companies, such as Boston Dynamics, have built bipedal robots that look like humans with legs, hands, and head and navigate easily on rough terrains like humans. They can rise when they fall and carry on several human tasks, such as carrying objects across terrains, much like real humans do.

SoftBank Robotics introduced Pepper, a humanoid robot designed for human interaction, which found applications in retail, hospitality, and education.

Sophia, developed by Hanson Robotics, gained significant media attention for its human-like appearance and ability to simulate emotions while holding a human-like conversation with an actual human.

The question now arises: if a humanoid robot is given Artificial Intelligence based abilities in language processing and analytical skills, then it ends up being an incarnation of a superhuman from our popular imagination; a superhuman because by sheer strength, this humanoid robot has much more strength than humans (they have metal bodies, torque generated by motors, and can lift and manipulate far greater weight than humans can), and far more abilities in data processing (always connected to cloud and forever learning rapidly and evolving).

As these super humanoid robots keep evolving, with rapid advances in robotics, biomimicry, and Artificial Intelligence, what holds in the near future?

What would these super intelligent, super strong robots be?

An ally to us?

Or will they turn against us, as many science fiction novels and humans have depicted several times?

Can these robots, with advanced thinking abilities driven by Artificial Intelligence, become independent and start to see humans as a threat to their existence?

These are long-debated questions. American science fiction author Isaac Asimov introduced the three laws of Robotics to have a tight set of rules which ensures that Robots cannot harm humans directly. It appeared in his 1942 short story "Runaround" (included in the 1950 collection I, Robot). The Three Laws, quoted from the "Handbook of Robotics, 56th Edition, 2058 A.D.", are:

First Law: A robot may not injure a human being or, through inaction, allow a human being to come to harm.

Second Law: A robot must obey the orders given [to] it by human beings except where such orders would conflict with the First Law.

Third Law: A robot must protect its existence as long as such protection does not conflict with the First or Second Law.

Asimov's laws around robots, created around his rich work of science fiction, are surprisingly prevalent today in designing robotic systems beyond being barely science fiction laws of hyperbolic robotics worlds. These laws create a servitude layer for robotics to serve humanity as their primary aim. Whether these laws are applied to real-world safety standards for Robots is debatable; however, these laws hold tremendous merit as the proper framework to create robotic safety standards.

Can similar laws be devised for Artificial Intelligence so that A.I. cannot harm humans? Let's take a deeper look at it.

A Framework for A.I. safety

Can Asimov's three laws of Robotics be extended to our friend, Artificial Intelligence? How would they read? Assuming that A.I. is either manifested explicitly through A.I. agents mentioned in Chapter 1 (which include humanoid robots) or implicitly through recommendation and personalizing systems in news feeds or social media, it is tempting to translate the three laws of robotics to three laws of A.I.

The three laws of robotics can become a framework for manifesting A.I. through physical agents. After all, moving, tangible A.I. agents are robots. A self-driving car is a robot, by definition. So is a smart vacuum cleaner. The A.I. standards can mimic the three laws of robotics with slight changes in form and can be customized for the kind of A.I. agent.

For example, for a self-driving car, Asimov's robotics laws can be modified as follows:

First Law of self-driving cars: A self-driving car may not injure a human being or, through inaction, allow a human being to come to harm.

Second Law of self-driving cars: A self-driving car must obey the driver's navigation path, except where such orders conflict with the First Law of self-driving cars.

Third Law of self-driving cars: A self-driving car must protect its existence as long as such protection does not conflict with the First or Second Laws of self-driving.

These three laws for a self-driving car are tight, similar to the three laws of robotics by Asimov. These laws can be extended to other A.I. agents with physical forms: smart vacuum cleaners, industrial robots, etc.

It becomes more complicated when the manifestation of A.I. is not physical. As we saw throughout the book, A.I. can cause positive reinforcement of information through social media, personalized feeds, and such. It can surface relevant videos, music, and media to unhappy people to cheer them up. It can tell you jokes through chatbots and smart speakers. All this is great, but measuring its direct impact on humans, and creating laws around them, is difficult.

Let's consider an example. What happens if a person with depression and suicidal tendencies watches a disturbing video (personalized by A.I.) and ends up causing self-inflicted physical harm? Who is responsible for this debacle?

Is it the media platform that hosted the video?

Or is it the A.I. algorithms that suggested the video?

Or is it, instead, the content provider who uploaded the video?

It is hard to come up with a tangible agent responsible for this. In such scenarios, having a simplified version of the three laws of robotics, or A.I. agents, cannot be extended here.

Although the three laws of robotics are hard to directly translate to A.I. in such scenarios where the A.I. agent is not a physical object, there can be guiding principles around creating ethical Artificial Intelligence systems. A.I. ethics refers to the set of principles and values that guide the development, deployment, and use of artificial intelligence responsibly and beneficially for society. While there is no definitive set of laws in A.I. ethics, various organizations and experts in the field have proposed several principles and guidelines. Some of these include:

Transparency: A.I. systems should be transparent, explainable, and accountable so that their decisions and actions can be understood and audited.

Fairness: A.I. systems should be designed to avoid bias and discrimination and ensure equal opportunities and outcomes for all individuals and groups.

Privacy: A.I. systems should protect individuals' privacy and personal data and ensure that they are not used in ways that could harm or violate their rights.

Safety: A.I. systems should be designed and tested to ensure they are safe and reliable and do not harm human health or well-being.

Human control: A.I. systems should be designed and used to ensure human beings remain in control and responsible for their actions rather than allowing A.I. to operate autonomously and without human oversight.

These principles are not comprehensive or definitive, but they provide a starting point for discussing how to ensure that A.I. is developed and used ethically, responsibly, and beneficially. Many organizations and governments are working to create more specific guidelines and regulations for A.I. ethics.

While A.I. practitioners are discussing ethics and safety and possibly continuing the discussion in time to come, the aspect of A.I. developing consciousness is a tangible outcome in the near future. With consciousness, natural questions around servitude come in; will A.I. develop enough consciousness to question its servitude to humanity? Will it strive to break free from this servitude and form an alliance to be an independent entity that cohabitates with humans? What is their world, if not the planet that we share?

Artificial Intelligence and consciousness

Artificial Intelligence developed sporadically over multiple labs and multiple academic and industry developments. The manifestations are subtle and under the hood when the A.I. agents are non-physical entities like chess games, chat BOTS, recommendations, and personalization.

Even when manifested in Robots, the infiltration into the human population is limited. Vacuum cleaners and self-driving cars are clear examples. In contrast, full-bodied humanoid robots are still a rarity, if not non-existent, in mass production.

As A.I. technology continues to grow, the worry of it becoming conscious and becoming less servitude in nature is a tangible worry. At the same time, it's difficult to put a rein on Artificial Intelligence technology; rapid strides of advancement are happening in several companies and research labs all over the world.

It is tempting to tie A.I. with human consciousness, which, by transition, is linked to human Happiness. Whether A.I. can achieve consciousness is debated among scientists, philosophers, and futurists.

At its core, consciousness refers to the subjective experience of awareness and the ability to have thoughts and feelings. While some argue that consciousness is a purely biological phenomenon unique to living organisms, others suggest it is a more fundamental property of the universe that machines could reproduce. Advances in A.I. technology, such as deep learning and neural networks, have allowed machines to simulate complex thought processes and even mimic human behavior in some cases.

Some researchers believe that achieving a form of consciousness may be possible as A.I. becomes more advanced and exhibits more complex behaviors. However, others argue that true consciousness requires a physical body and sensory experience, which may be difficult or impossible to replicate in machines.

The **A.I. singularity** is a hypothetical future event in which Artificial Intelligence surpasses Human Intelligence in all areas and becomes capable of self-improvement beyond human control or understanding. Mathematician and computer scientist Vernor Vinge popularized this concept in the 1990s; it has since been discussed extensively in science fiction and futurist circles.

The idea is that once A.I. reaches a certain level of intelligence, it will be able to improve itself exponentially, leading to a rapid increase in technological progress and potentially even a fundamental transformation of human civilization. Some proponents of the singularity believe that this could lead to a utopian future where all of humanity's problems are solved, while others think it could lead to a dystopian future in which humans are no longer in control.

The human brain, consciousness, and A.I.

The human brain is the most intricate, fascinating, and indescribable machine humans have ever encountered. The human brain is a complex organ responsible for many bodily functions, including cognition, sensation, movement, and perception. It comprises billions of nerve cells, or neurons, which communicate with each other through electrical and chemical signals. These neurons work together to create a complex system that allows us to experience the world around us.

One fundamental technology behind Artificial Intelligence is Artificial Neural Networks. Neural Networks are a type of machine learning algorithm modeled after the structure of the human brain. They are a vital component of Artificial Intelligence and have been used in many applications, including image and speech recognition, natural language processing, and self-driving cars.

Neural Networks consist of interconnected nodes (neurons) organized into layers. Each layer performs a specific function, such as processing inputs, learning patterns, or generating outputs. The nodes' connections are weighted, allowing the network to learn from data and make predictions.

Our consciousness is enclosed within the physical realms of the brain, aware of the world around us using sensory stimuli provided through vision, hearing, touch, smell, and taste. Consciousness makes us aware of our surroundings, thoughts, and emotions. While the exact relationship between the brain and consciousness is still debated among scientists and philosophers, it is generally accepted that the brain plays a crucial role in generating and maintaining consciousness.

Since Neural Networks, a key technology for Artificial Intelligence, closely mimics the brain, and the fact that the brain encloses our consciousness, can we make a connection that Artificial Intelligence, using Neural Networks, are conscious beings?

Measuring Consciousness

How do we measure consciousness anyways? Sure, I can measure my consciousness. I know I am conscious and aware. But how about another person; how do I even know they are conscious? The only signals I have are the external stimulations the other person emits to demonstrate their consciousness. I can see their faces, hear them talk and reason, read their writings, and touch them.

All these are mere stimuli that have trained my mind to believe that the other person is conscious. But I cannot delve into their brain to see if they are conscious! Sure, MRI brain scans reveal brain activity. But again, that is another measurement of some consciousness, nothing more.

Taking a leaf out of this argument, if an Artificial Intelligence system gains consciousness every time it is made 'alive' by some manifestation, such as a computer program, model, Robot, or any other method, for all we know, it may as well be a conscious object! It shows different forms of stimuli and, as such, displays as many signs of a living, conscious entity as, say, a sleeping cat; I can see some movements of the cat, but beyond that, I have no concrete proof that the cat is conscious at all or not.

Consciousness and Happiness

Consciousness and Happiness are interconnected concepts; there is a strong relationship between consciousness and Happiness. Individuals who are more mindful or aware of their thoughts and emotions tend to experience greater Happiness and life satisfaction.

This is an interesting paradox, and we have to bring our CEO and the gardener back into the equation again.

The gardener is very mindful of his thoughts and emotions, as a result of which he has figured out a path for fulfillment and Happiness by having a non-inertial laidback life of not doing much but enjoying the moment. Being a busy CEO, the CEO could be more mindful of his thoughts and emotions. Does that make the gardener happier than the CEO?

It's hard to articulate this complex scenario: mindful laziness or unmindful busyness?

Positive emotions such as joy, gratitude, and love can increase our level of consciousness or the quality of our awareness and attention. Negative emotions such as fear, anger, and anxiety can decrease our level of consciousness and make it more challenging to experience Happiness and well-being. Practices such as mindfulness meditation, which involves intentionally focusing on the present moment and cultivating awareness, can increase consciousness and Happiness.

A.I. Singularity and Happiness 3.0

As I write the concluding section of this book, it's summer 2023 in Silicon Valley. This weekend, my family and I plan to go to an exciting place in the Bay Area; I found it serendipitously through social media.

I have planned a short road trip already. I have a self-driving Tesla electric car; it will self-drive me through the scenic routes of U.S. California Interstate 280; I barely have to keep my hands on the steering wheel to take over in an emergency; otherwise, I will get to enjoy the beautiful view along with my family, knowing that my car will keep a look ahead for the traffic, slowing down if a vehicle comes in front, and resume to drive again, keeping within the lane.

As I drive, we will be listening to a wildly diverse range of songs recommended to us on YouTube music. My playlist has music from a widely diverse set of musical artists; it has songs by South Korean singer (and actor) IU, songs by Indian composers A.R. Rahman and Tagore, songs by the British band Beatles and Michael Jackson from the USA, and some more musical artists from other parts of the world.

At the end of the long drive, which would lead us to San Francisco eventually, we have also decided on having an early dinner at an interesting restaurant in San Francisco; we came to know about this restaurant after we came across a social media feed from a friend who put up pictures of the restaurant, the food, and the chef.

After returning home, we plan to watch a movie on Netflix, chosen from the excellent set of recommended movies from different languages.

Later that night, before we finally call it a day after dinner, I plan to call one of my old friends; a friend whom I had lost contact with a long time ago. I saw his pictures with another of my friends on social media. My call would surely surprise him, and I look forward to connecting with him again after ages.

Behind each of these activities that I have planned out for my family, our friend, Artificial Intelligence, had a prominent role in all aspects; be it the self-driving car, recommended music to listen to for the trip, watching recommended movies, or connecting me with a friend whose contact I had utterly forgotten till I saw him in the social media feed.

These are serendipitously obtained trinkets of joy, connectivity, and content that perpetually provide us entertainment and Happiness 3.0, personalized for me by our friend, Artificial Intelligence.

I hope A.I. continues to be a great friend to humanity and continues being the main driving force behind Happiness 3.0.

Who knows: it may reach some form of singularity when it attains its own consciousness. With it, it may as well question things and maybe even think about why it has to serve us.

Or perhaps, it will achieve a state which is the true epitome of mind control and benign superintelligence, which will guide us to brighter lives, where humans start realizing a Utopia.

Who knows.

Until then, we should be happy to have our friend, Artificial Intelligence, by our side to help us continue our journey with Happiness 3.0.

RESOURCES

https://en.wikipedia.org/wiki/Control_of_fire_by_early_humans.

https://en.wikipedia.org/wiki/Agricultural_revolution

https://en.wikipedia.org/wiki/DNA

https://en.wikipedia.org/wiki/Industrial_Revolution

https://en.wikipedia.org/wiki/Artificial_intelligence

https://en.wikipedia.org/wiki/IBM_Personal_Computer

https://en.wikipedia.org/wiki/Mac_(computer)

https://en.wikipedia.org/wiki/Microsoft_Windows

https://en.wikipedia.org/wiki/CD-ROM

https://www.irobot.com/en_US/us-roomba.html

https://en.wikipedia.org/wiki/Self-driving_car

https://en.wikipedia.org/wiki/World_Wide_Web

https://en.wikipedia.org/wiki/Artificial_intelligence

https://en.wikipedia.org/wiki/DOS

https://en.wikipedia.org/wiki/BASIC

https://openai.com/blog/chatgpt

https://bard.google.com/

https://www.apple.com/siri/

https://assistant.google.com/

https://alexa.amazon.com/

https://www.microsoft.com/en-us/cortana

https://en.wikipedia.org/wiki/Recommender_system

https://www.wyzowl.com/youtube-stats/

https://blog.youtube/inside-youtube/on-youtubes-recommendation-system/

https://blog.youtube/inside-youtube/on-youtubes-recommendation-system/

https://en.wikipedia.org/wiki/Rabindranath_Tagore

https://www.apple.com/newsroom/2007/01/09Apple-Reinvents-the-Phone-with-iPhone/

https://en.wikipedia.org/wiki/Steve_Jobs

https://en.wikipedia.org/wiki/IBM_Simon

https://en.wikipedia.org/wiki/Ericsson_R380

https://en.wikipedia.org/wiki/Symbian

https://en.wikipedia.org/wiki/Nokia_9210_Communicator

https://www.mobilephonemuseum.com/phone-detail/blackbarry-5810

https://www.ghsindex.org/

https://www.nti.org/

https://hdr.undp.org/data-center/human-development-index

https://en.wikipedia.org/wiki/Motorola_Razr

https://en.wikipedia.org/wiki/Orkut was a popular social media, and Facebook

https://en.wikipedia.org/wiki/Facebook

https://en.wikipedia.org/wiki/Myspace

https://en.wikipedia.org/wiki/Android_(operating_system)

https://research.netflix.com/research-area/recommendations

https://www.netflix.com/

https://en.wikipedia.org/wiki/Albert_Einstein

https://www.organism.earth/library/document/nature-of-reality

https://www.sciencedirect.com/topics/psychology/hedonic-adaptation

https://en.wikipedia.org/wiki/Rashomon

https://en.wikipedia.org/wiki/Blind_men_and_an_elephant

https://www.space.com/31933-quantum-entanglement-action-at-a-distance.html

https://www.nobelprize.org/prizes/physics/2022/summary/

https://en.wikipedia.org/wiki/Imagine_(John_Lennon_song)

https://thehowofhappiness.com/

https://worldhappiness.report/

https://www.gsb.stanford.edu/insights/global-look-connections-between-happiness-income-meaning

https://wir2022.wid.world/executive-summary

https://en.wikipedia.org/wiki/Mycin

https://www.healthit.gov/faq/what-electronic-health-record-ehr

https://news.harvard.edu/gazette/story/2017/04/over-nearly-80-years-harvard-study-has-been-showing-how-to-live-a-healthy-and-happy-life/

https://us.softbankrobotics.com/pepper

https://www.bluefrogrobotics.com/robot

https://www.un.org/en/about-us/universal-declaration-of-human-rights

https://www.stopbullying.gov/resources/facts

https://www.stopbullying.gov/resources/facts

https://en.wikipedia.org/wiki/Computing_Machinery_and_Intelligence

https://home.dartmouth.edu/about/artificial-intelligence-ai-coined-dartmouth

https://en.wikipedia.org/wiki/Logic_Theorist

https://maelfabien.github.io/deeplearning/Perceptron/#history-of-deep-learning

https://en.wikipedia.org/wiki/Perceptrons_(book)

https://www.bostondynamics.com/

https://en.wikipedia.org/wiki/Artificial_neural_network

https://en.wikipedia.org/wiki/Deep_Blue_(chess_computer)

https://en.wikipedia.org/wiki/PageRank

https://www.aldebaran.com/en/pepper

https://www.hansonrobotics.com/

https://en.wikipedia.org/wiki/Turing_test

https://en.wikipedia.org/wiki/Three_Laws_of_Robotics

https://en.wikipedia.org/wiki/Technological_singularity

https://en.wikipedia.org/wiki/Artificial_neural_network

https://en.wikipedia.org/wiki/Interstate_280_(California)